The Orchards
of Perseverance

The Orchards
of Perseverance

Conversations with Trappist Monks
About God, Their Lives, and the World

by
David D. Perata

St. Therese's Press
P.O. Box 10, Ruthven, Iowa 51358

Nihil Obstat:
  Rev. Msgr. James K. Lafferty, Ph.D
Imprimatur:
  +Daniel N. DiNardo, D.D.
  Bishop of Sioux City, Iowa
February 28, 2002

Permissions and Credits:

Excerpts from *The Waters of Siloe*, copyright 1949 by Thomas Merton and renewed 1977 by The Trustees of the Merton Legacy Trust, reprinted by permission of Harcourt, Inc.

Excerpts from *The Cistercian Way* by André Louf, © 1989; *Cistercian Communio* by Thomas X. Davis, Cistercian Studies Quarterly, © 1994; *Thomas Merton On St. Bernard* by Thomas Merton, © 1980; *The Letters of Adam of Perseigne*, tr. Grace Perigo, intro by Thomas Merton, Cistercian Father Series 21, © 1976; reprinted by permission of Cistercian Publications, Kalamazoo, Michigan-Spencer, Massachusetts.

Published in the United States of America
by St. Therese's Press, P.O. Box 10, Ruthven, Iowa 51358

Library of Congress Catalog Card Number: 99-71204
ISBN 0-9672135-0-9

Library of Congress Cataloging-in-Publication Data
Perata, David D.
    The orchards of perseverance : conversations with Trappist monks about God, their lives, and the world / David D. Perata. — 1st ed.
    p. cm.
    Includes bibliographical references and index.
    LCCN: 99-71204
    ISBN: 0-9672135-0-9

    1. Abbey of Our Lady of New Clairvaux (Vina, Calif.) 2. Trappists—Interviews. 3. Vina (Calif.)—Church history—20th century.
I. Title.

BX2525.A33P47 1999   271'.125079427
                         QBI99-1101

Cover Design by Smollett Design
Interior design and production by Steve German PhotoGraphics
All photos by the author except where otherwise noted

Printed and bound in the United States of America.

♻ Printed on recycled paper

T his book is lovingly dedicated
to the following people -

To my mom and dad, Richard and Theresa Perata, for raising
me in the faith and providing a firm spiritual foundation upon
which my life has been built. They never ceased to support
me in my endeavors, and in retrospect at their recent
departure from this world, I see them as two of my best
friends. I know they continue to help me from their spiritual
home, and I hope they are pleased.

To my wife Pamela and daughter Cheyenne, whose love has
seen me through the difficult times. I love you both so very,
very much! God has truly blessed me with your presence in
my life.

To Joe, my lifelong soul mate and the other member of Chow
(Clark wink), whose childhood and young adult life he shared
with me. It was he who introduced me to New Clairvaux,
and he with whom I shared the joys and pains of youth.
With love, May God Bless You as I've been blessed.

And to all the monks at New Clairvaux who patiently
allowed this intrusion into their otherwise private lives -
whether included in the book or not - I extend my heartfelt
thanks for allowing this project to see the light of day. I can
only hope that you are pleased with the fruit of this harvest.

A special hello to my old pal Brother Adam, who has joined
the ranks of saints and who, I'm sure, is bending the ear of
some archangel standing by the Pearly Gates.

Acknowledgements

I am greatly indebted to all the people who have helped to make this book happen.

First and foremost, to Abbot Thomas Davis and novice master Father Paul Mark of the Abbey of Our Lady of New Clairvaux monastery, who lovingly guided me through this spiritual journey. Through countless meetings, discussions and late-night e-mails, our friendship has grown to a new level of honesty and intimacy that held me together during the difficult times with this project. Fortunately for me, they both shared an appreciation for my views on life and sense of humor, and their compassion for the darker side of our humanness provided an unconditional ground for me when my vision became blurred. Their support and assistance as spiritual advisors for the content of this book greatly influenced and shaped what you are about to read. I am genuinely blessed to call these men my friends.

There are numerous friends and colleagues who read through the manuscript during its early stages and provided invaluable insights and opinions as to its final content. I thank all of you for your time and thoughts, and especially your friendship and support.

Thanks to Steve German for his uncanny ability to take ideas and turn them into the finished pages that you see here before you. I thank him for his patience with me during the entire design process, and providing me with options — always options!

And to Laurie Smollet for her wonderful cover design! Laurie and I go back a number of years, and she understands and tolerates my method of working pretty well. When I push the creative envelope far past what is called for, she always allows me the necessary space to achieve my visions without compromise. A giving and compassionate spirit, I thank her for her unselfish friendship, talent, and support during this project.

Thank you Donna Crilly at Paulist Press for your acute copy editing skills.

Finally, in attempting a project such as this, there are always the unsung individuals at organizations and companies across the country who, at one time or another, have provided answers to the many questions I have asked. It might have been through a proper letter, or even an impromptu phone call, but so many have graciously lent their time and expertise in areas that were unfamiliar to me. I thank all of you.

Contents

Foreword

Reading interviews given by monastics is frequently accompanied by a nagging curiosity to know if these people are normal or not. If the decision is they're "normal," curiosity — yet unsatisfied — still asks "why are they living such a strange life?" However, if they're *not* "normal" people, curiosity still remains unsatisfied, now pondering "what more can be uncovered?"

The Orchards of Perseverence isn't meant to address curiosity; it addresses a call from God. The Bible presents God to us as a God who calls us. This book is about men called by God, about the way they perceived their God calling them, and about their responses to their divine call.

In their interviews, my brother monks present a remarkable vision of God with all the splendor they bring to their lives by responding to this vision: "Here I am." Each of my brothers relates his growing awareness of how in his personal life — regardless of how dark, fragile and human it may be — he has come to see his life as the life of God. A sense of self emerges. Consequently, they have a story to tell and a life to love and live. The message in their respective visions of God is not that God is to be sought outside of the self. Rather, they come to experience the teaching of Bernard of Clairvaux and William of St. Thierry that just as the soul is the life of the body, so God is the life of the soul. Otherwise, God could not have called them.

As an understanding of the presence of God comes to light, this light, in turn, can be blinding — even bringing darkness. This is the darkness of God's presence, dark because it is happening by the divine call; humanly speaking, it doesn't make any sense. It is incomprehensible that God uses one's human life, all the deep movements of the human spirit — even those darkest moments of brokenness and despair — to call that person. The divine call asks the surrender of the self to God. As these personal stories unfold, one can see that the brothers are bold enough to make this gift of themselves to the divine.

The Orchards of Perseverance

Why publish personal interviews from Trappist monks, known for their withdrawal from society? David, the author of this book, with his long-standing relationship with our community — some thirty years now — is well-acquainted with some of the brothers and has a good grasp of our way of life. He asked us to share our experiences of what it means to encounter God calling one to the monastic way and remaining faithful to the call and the life. Such encounters and fidelity do not exist without results and commitments to an Order and spiritual path.

David offers insights into the Order's spirituality and history. He opens up a practical approach towards understanding how monastic theology is alive and wedded to the ordinary daily life of the brothers. With his keen perception, David has been able to make this presentation in language that is easy to follow. We, David and the brothers, hope that if just one person from among the many who will read this book comes away from it with a better and healthier sense of direction for his or her own life's issues, if that person can begin to see God or Christ in a new perspective even in a divine darkness, then this sharing of personal mysteries of life has been worth it. For Christ, the Son of God, is to be glorified in all things.

Thomas X. Davis,
Abbot of New Clairvaux
January 9, 1999

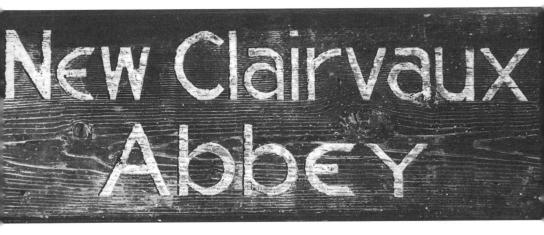

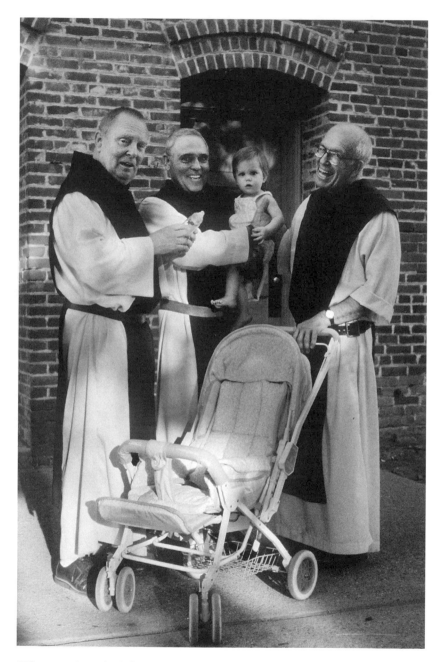

"Three monks and a baby! Brothers John Cullen, Pierre and Paul Bernard with the author's daughter Cheyenne."

Introduction

I am sitting in room fourteen of an old guest house named St. Matthew at the Abbey of Our Lady of New Clairvaux monastery in Vina, California, having been rousted from my bed at four-thirty in the morning by thoughts too stirring to allow sleep. A train whistle echoes off in the distance, adding excitement to the night in pretty much the same way that it did some thirty years ago, when I was a kid staying in this very same room. I cannot help but think back on how I ever found this place, and the incredible road that has led to this very moment.

In June of 1967, I climbed down the vestibule steps of a northbound passenger train into a balmy summer evening in California's Sacramento Valley. The chirping of crickets greeted me as the red tail light of the streamliner *Cascade* disappeared into the sunset. Glancing toward the ancient yellow depot, I spotted my best friend Joe, his brother Ed and their dad waiting for me on the station platform.

The excitement of the train ride and the adventure of these strange, new surroundings was somewhat inhibited by the obvious displeasure of Joe's father as we all piled into the car for the brief ride to the monastery. You see, Joe's dad really wasn't too keen on my coming to the abbey. He knew all too well that the combination of two seventh-grade boys wasn't always conducive to peaceful surroundings. Well hey, Joe and I loved to laugh — an awful lot! Actually, it seemed we laughed our way through childhood together. After all, isn't that what a child is supposed to do? We had a lot of innocent, if sometimes mischievous, fun.

But the fact was, I kinda went behind Joe's dad's back when I wrote to Father Joseph at the monastery to ask permission to come for a visit. School had barely let out for summer that year when Joe announced to me that he was going to a monastery with his dad for a few weeks. I was crushed! My best friend leaving for who-knew-how-long to live with a bunch of Trappist monks right when summer was beginning! What

The guest house area in 1956. Although the fence had been removed, this is basically how it looked when the author arrived in 1967.

kind of fun was that?

I soon found out what kind of fun. The stories that Joe wrote home to me about monks letting him drive jeeps and tractors, hunting rabbits and having prune fights on their 450 acres of prune and walnut orchards sounded more like a boys' summer camp than a monastery. It sounded too good for me to be sitting home alone. The only thing to do was to try and get there myself. But his dad had said "no way" in a big way. I guess it might have been kind of bold for me to go behind his back, but I did. And boy, my life would never be the same!

And so it was with some surprise and no small measure of displeasure that Joe's father — a strict yet lovely German man — gave me the cold shoulder for most of the car ride back to the monastery that evening. Now that I think about it, he did for most of the two weeks I was to stay at New Clairvaux that first time. But when I caught sight of the large, white wooden cross standing in a field beside the private road leading onto the monastic grounds, I didn't much care about all that. It was truly a magical experience! The sun had set, and the aroma of freshly cut alfalfa hung in the warm night air like a perfume amidst the darkness of the monastery. Old board and batten guest houses, built decades earlier when the monastery was a vineyard owned by rail mogul and California politician Leland Stanford, stood silently in a row along the right side of the tree-lined pavement. And just as Joe's dad had feared, the exuberance of youth got the best of us as we darted through the trees in the

The same view in 1999. The new guest house building is set back from the road.

blackness, Joe proudly showing me around this new territory that he was sharing with me for the first time.

The cover of night added a definite element of mystery as Joe led the way to the old winery building, a huge brick affair built in 1887 which formerly housed vats of wine when Stanford grew grapes out in the fertile fields. The structure was now inhabited by John Deeres, Farmalls, cars, harvesters, shakers, low boys, trucks and an assortment of hand-me-down farming equipment, including the two infamous army surplus jeeps — one yellow and one green — that would become our personal transportation around the grounds for the duration of my stay. Two kids on acres and acres of prune and walnut orchards, dirt roads, jeeps, no parents (well, one); it was a heady experience for a seventh grader. Needless to say, we had a blast!

Coming out of strong and fairly strict Catholic families, the monastic values and lifestyle turned out to be a breath of fresh air from the more fear-driven Catholicism we had experienced in Catholic schools. We'd caught the tail end of Catholic grammar school when nuns still outnumbered lay teachers, and the parish pastor came into every grade to pass out report cards in front of the entire class. Naturally, we were raised to hold all religious people in high esteem, even awe, and now here we found ourselves among thirty-five monks who were in perhaps the most traditionally mysterious of all religious orders.

And yet there was no extraordinary difference between the monks and us kids. They worked; we worked. They prayed; we prayed. Maybe it was that for the first time we saw the religious with their collars removed, so-to-speak. We had rarely had a chance to see a priest or a nun in secular clothes, or sipping a beer, or working on a tractor. There had always been the illusion that the collar or the habit maintained, which kept a division between the laity and the clergy. At New Clairvaux, that was all broken down, and we could see these monks simply acting as human beings in blue jeans and work shirts, who put on the cowl when it was

This 1955 aerial view shows the enormity of the winery building. The guest houses can be seen behind the upper right corner of the winery.

time to pray. We saw a side of religious life we had never seen before. Perhaps the biggest novelty was that they treated us with great respect and trust. I wouldn't say we were exactly equals, but they sure did seem to appreciate the enthusiasm and innocence of our youth.

Of course, it is quite possible that we somewhat took advantage of our new-found freedom. That summer, Joe and I weren't the only kids staying in the guest houses. There were two brothers and their two friends — all older than we were — who had a Chevy wagon at their disposal with the first eight-track stereo I had ever seen or heard. We'd frequently sneak out of the monastery grounds in the evening and cruise the local small-town hamburger drive-ins with their assortment of what we called "rednecks" and cute young country girls. Or maybe we'd attempt to sleep in the tree house that was built in an old oak tree near Deer Creek, or have prune fights with the monks over at the dehydrator, or hunt rabbits in the orchards by jeep with Brother Pierre.

About the only time the monks ever expressed real disapproval with any of us was when Joe and I painted the railroad bridge on the edge of the property in psychedelic colors, with paints acquired from the monastery garage!

The Southern Pacific Railroad took a rather dim view of our exploits, and went straight to the monks for an explanation. Why go to the monks? Well, it seems that some high-spirited youths from town had come and poured red paint all over our brightly colored "hippie artwork." We were so incensed that we communicated our displeasure to them via painted excerpts from the Scriptures, written on the side of the bridge abutment in red paint. One particularly catchy phrase that is still faintly visible on the bridge is, "Father forgive them, they know not what they do."

I suppose the religious overtones of the work did point a finger to the monastery. As a result, the verdict came down that I was a bad influence on Joe and would not be permitted to come up for awhile until things cooled off. I can't recall exactly how long it was that I was refused admittance, but eventually I worked my way back in. Today, this is a rather well-known story that never fails to raise a smile on the monks' faces when mentioned.

When I arrived at the monastery it was *the* summer of the sixties: The "Summer of Love." The Beatles were the major force in music and the reverberations of Vatican II had reached the desolate confines of New Clairvaux like an atomic bomb. Although we were too young to know it at the time, the abbey was dangerously close to shutting down. Those monks who couldn't adapt to the changes ushered in by Vatican II left the monastery, and there were many. In retrospect, the laid-back feeling of the monastery during this period that allowed us so much freedom was in actuality an indication that things were not as they should be.

Fortunately, the Holy Spirit guided New Clairvaux through the sixties and they recovered. Over the next thirty-odd years, the monastery in Vina has been the most consistent thread running through my life year after year. These monks have seen me grow from a young kid on into a man, and all the triumphs and failures in between. Likewise, I've seen them grow from young men earnestly persevering in the life to seasoned monks who have grown wiser with the passing of years. Some have already died, all of them I call my friends; a handful are very close to me.

I could never quite seem to shake off the spirituality of New Clairvaux, being drawn there for a retreat at least once every year or two.

For many years it would still be Joe and I making the trip together, taking a break from writing songs and playing clubs in the San Francisco Bay area. The monks listened to our demo tapes with great enthusiasm, chiding us about the day we'd drive through the monastery gate in our Rolls Royce! And I'll never forget the morning we played the Beatles' "Here Comes The Sun" in church, our two acoustic guitars sounding like a symphony as the music reverberated off the stark plywood walls in the dawn's light. But even after Joe and I got married and went our separate ways, I would return to the monastery alone on many occasions to unwind from the worries of the world.

Early in 1991, I approached Abbot Thomas Davis about an idea I had to photograph the monastic life at New Clairvaux, along with interviewing the monks about their lives. At the time I didn't realize what I was asking. These are private men who shun publicity by the very nature of the *Rule of St. Benedict,* and guard their privacy very carefully. The last thing in the world a monk wants is a camera shoved in his face or a microphone set before him. But in my ignorance I gained entry, presumably because of my close ties with the community over the years. The abbot very graciously consented to the intrusion, giving me carte blanche in interviewing and photographing the monastic life at New Clairvaux. I sought to somehow catch the essence of these monks and New Clairvaux in words and photos, and so began interviewing them in-depth on all facets of their life from their calling to the present day.

A series of articles was written from the interviews, but the complete oral histories lay silent for nearly seven years until I came across them while rummaging through some old boxes one afternoon. I began reading them all over again. They were still as fresh and inspiring as the day they were recorded. In the course of these intimate conversations, the monks discussed leaving loved ones and civilian life to answer the call from God, and the tests of faith along that road. They addressed the loneliness of the novitiate, where many monks arrive at the brink of insanity as they meet themselves perhaps for the first time.

The monks also talked about the mystical aspects of a relationship with God, and how and if they know God answers. Is it a one way street or do they actually know God's communicating? And how do they view life outside the monastery gate? It was the first time in my association with the monastery that I had actually sat down with a number of the monks on a one-to-one basis and asked all the personal questions that I, and no doubt countless others, have wondered about this supposedly mysterious lifestyle.

Perhaps what sticks out in my mind the most over the years is that the monks never preached or condescended to us. They have a broad tolerance for human foibles, and look more for the basic goodness in humankind rather than our sinfulness. And because the monks are sequestered more or less out of the mainstream of society, they aren't prey to all the vanities and excesses that plague most of us. As a result, their approach to life and their amusement and compassion for *our* lifestyle is every bit as incredible as some people's misgivings about *theirs*.

I've heard some people comment that they think the monks are copping out on life by hiding away in a monastery, that somehow they're not contributing to the world. But to foster such an attitude, one has to disallow the power of prayer or the monks' own rights as human beings to relate to God as they are called. These men sincerely believe that they have the greatest outreach to the world in the monastery through prayer.

At the time that I rediscovered the interviews, I was in the middle of a novel that I was quite excited about. But for some reason, I felt that I should stop and make these interviews available to the public. I immediately contacted Abbot Thomas Davis at New Clairvaux and told him about my idea to do a book of the monks oral histories. He was very enthusiastic about the prospect, and we arranged a meeting along with Father Paul Mark, the novice master, to discuss the approach and what message we envisioned this book conveying to people.

Out of that meeting came the major focus of this project: To humanize the monk and lift the cloak of mystery from the monastic lifestyle. And rather than take an academic approach to the subject matter, they allowed me the freedom to write the book simply through the eyes of my own experience.

It has been an extremely intense undertaking, much more so than I would ever have imagined. What I found while researching the history of Cistercian monasticism was an incredible description of the mystical relationship between God and the human soul, and how a monk strives to perfect this relationship through his monastic vocation. To put it in the vernacular, it simply blew my mind! Suddenly there was an entirely new aspect to Christianity than simply going to Mass on Sunday and living the commandments. If you pierce through all the surface amenities that we are accustomed to — statues, paintings, ornamentation, singing and the rituals themselves — and penetrate deeper into the life of Christ, you will find a mystical realm that delves into the very depths of our spiritual existence.

The Orchards of Perseverance will hopefully serve as a source of inspiration for everyone, especially those who may be going through a crisis in faith or are considering a religious vocation. It's also a good starting point toward investigating a more mystical spirituality. A bibliography at the end of this book offers excellent reading for those who wish to pursue the mystical approach to God through Christ.

    I sincerely hope that the reader will come away with something positive that they can use in their daily life. After all, if you want your car fixed, go to an auto mechanic. If you want to learn about the mystical aspects of a life with God, listen to those who have devoted their entire lives to the quest.

† † †

New Clairvaux Archives

My dear friend Joe with his dad and the infamous yellow jeep.

Cistercian History

The roots of modern monasticism can be traced directly to ancient Egypt of the third and fourth centuries, where men and women who sought refuge and solitude from the noise and confusion of the world fled into the arid deserts or cooler mountain regions to live as hermits.[1] Scripture tells us that Christ often went out into the desert for extended periods of prayer.

A person can also find anonymity by getting lost within a crowd, and one of the earliest major cenobitic (common life) monasteries, founded by St. Pachomius at Tabennisi, in Egypt, provided such an opportunity to lose one's self amidst a community of perhaps several thousand, who lived a regimented and somewhat dehumanized life of hard labor.

These separate and very distinct lifestyles provide the two basic expressions of monasticism that — with modification and reform over the centuries — have evolved into what has become known as the Order of Cistercians of the Strict Observance, or Trappists.

The hermits and cenobites of ancient Egypt were not originally referred to as *monks*. The term *ascetic*, meaning "one in training," was commonly given to the early Christians who lived the solitary life, whether within the Christian community or set apart. Women who lived this same lifestyle were called *consecrated virgins*. And because the Church during this period favored communal liturgical worship, it disapproved of those who ventured out on their own to live the ascetic life. The term *monk*, which was derived from the Greek word *monachos*, originally referred to celibacy, and was not extensively used until monasticism gained widespread acceptance in the Christian world.

The concept of monasticism spread quickly throughout Europe due, in large part, to the writings of St. Athanasius. His widely read book, *The Life of St. Anthony*, told of the hermit whose complete transformation in the Egyptian desert amazed those who saw him emerge twenty years later as a perfect example of spiritual peace. It defined the solitary life of the

1

monk and removed the mistrust and apprehension that had previously been associated with the title of *monk*. The word now took on the meaning of a Christian who lived a solitary life devoted to God.

For some monks, monasticism by the end of the fourth century was often a type of physical endurance test. Fasting, hard labor and self-mortification fostered subtle competitions between community members and concentrated on the exterior life of the monk. Simultaneously, the writings of Basil the Great, John Cassian, Evagrius and other great monastics — including Benedict of Nurisa at a later date — kept the focus on the interior life, or as the Trappist monk and writer Thomas Merton put it, "from the flesh to the will."

While a young student in Rome, St. Benedict had found city life distasteful and set out to live alone in the region of Subiaco. His solitude was short-lived, however, for he was discovered and asked to instruct others in his Christian solitude. What transpired was the formation of twelve groups of men that Benedict established in the hills overlooking Subiaco. Benedict was forced to move his group to Monte Cassino, where he founded a monastery and wrote his *Rule for Monasteries*, referred to as the *Rule of St. Benedict*, the very foundation of the Cistercian life.

St. Benedict wrote his *Rule* as an adaptation from a number of sources, among them a compilation of monastic traditions known as *The Rule of the Master*, written around the year 500 by an unknown author. Benedict whittled down its lengthy, drawn out traditions and observances until the average man or woman could abide by its usages without having to be a spiritual athlete. Thomas Merton describes some of the differences between former monastic practices and the new *Rule* prescribed by St. Benedict:

> His monks had plenty to eat and plenty of time to sleep. He reduced the choral offices of the Egyptians by about two thirds and sent the community out to work in the fields for seven or eights hours a day. Extraordinary mortifications were forbidden or discouraged. Virtue consisted in not attracting attention rather than in doing things that were conspicuous. The sacrifices that really mattered to him were those that were exacted in secrecy from the deepest veins of selfhood. . . One of Benedict's secrets was to purify the hearts of men by acts that were outwardly ordinary, simple, insignificant: the common lot of men, one's daily work, the petty business of getting along peacefully with other people.[2]

Along with these changes came the infusion of a deep and personal mystical relationship with God the Father through Jesus Christ and the

Scriptures. With Christ at the center of the *Rule*, and the focus placed on prayer, solitude and contemplation, the *Rule of St. Benedict* became what has been referred to as "the single and most powerful influential document of the monastic tradition in the western Church."[3]

The *Rule of St. Benedict* is a very detailed description of usages and observances to be used as a guideline for the monastic life. But as André Louf notes in *The Cistercian Way*, it is much more than that:

> . . . it is not enough to say that the text of the Rule contains a summary of the principals of the monastic life. Neither is it enough to claim that it faithfully traces the main characteristics of the kind of life that history has considered to be authentically monastic. The Rule is always more than a code of life or a manual of doctrine, although it is both of these. It is above all a resume of a spiritual experience that lies at the heart of monastic life. The principles of doctrine it evokes, or the details of observance which are recommended or even imposed by it, have an inner power. This power is an experience of the very life of God in Christ Jesus and His Holy Spirit. No rule has any other meaning than to be this path of life. . . .[4]

Over time even Benedict's *Rule* became diluted with compromise. Knights and noblemen took their solemn vows alongside the common man, resulting in unbalanced communities that were oftentimes rather rough around the edges. The original spirit of the *Rule* began to lose its uniformity, softening the lives of some monks while intensifying it for others. Social and political influences also began creeping into the monastery, and by the end of the seventh century monasticism in Europe was in a state of disarray.

There were, however, spirited reform movements that sprang up at various intervals during the eighth and ninth centuries which sustained monasticism through hard times in Europe. One of the more notable of these was Cluny, founded in 909/910. Situated in Burgundy, France, the monastery was started by a handful of monks under the spiritual direction of St. Berno. With Cluny, as with monasticism in general heading into the eleventh century, the *Rule* as prescribed by Benedict continued to experience a gradual transformation with each new reform that attempted to interpret its original spirit. There existed a clear division as to how the *Rule* was to be lived: Some favored a stricter lifestyle, others less so. With the death of St. Benedict around 547, it was left solely up to the abbots of the various monasteries to pass the *Rule* along to each succeeding generation.

For the most part it was well preserved, or it never would have survived. Yet, as with all traditions throughout history, the further removed one becomes from the source, the more a tradition loses its original intent. Such was the case with the *Rule*, and it wasn't until the eleventh century that the Holy Spirit intervened in a truly magnificent way.

A group of Benedictine monks in a French monastery at Molesme, in 1098, had become increasingly dissatisfied with the interpretation of the *Rule* in their community. The abbot, an elderly monk named Robert who possessed an acute power of spiritual discernment, concurred with those brothers who favored leaving Molesme to start their own reform. So on Palm Sunday of that same year, amidst the marshlands near Dijon, Robert and twenty-two monks from the abbey at Molseme founded a new monastery which would later come to be known as *Cîteaux*.

"The most ancient documents of Cîteaux," says Louf, "tell us that the desire of these men was to seek God in a desert place, in true poverty, in real independence of the secular establishment, and in greater fidelity to the *Rule of St. Benedict.*"[5] Their constitution strictly adhered to the *Rule of St. Benedict*, throwing out excess ornamentation in the church and returning prayer, meals, and work periods to the austere ideal laid out by Benedict at Monte Cassino over five hundred years before.

But the monks left behind at Molesme didn't understand the underlying reasons for the new reform at Cîteaux and petitioned Rome to force Robert back to Molesme to remain as their abbot. Reluctantly, Robert returned, leaving a prior by the name of Alberic in charge at Cîteaux. Under Alberic's direction — having to contend with the inhospitable environment and lack of understanding within certain groups — Cîteaux barely managed to sustain itself and attracted few new members. In time Alberic's successor, Stephen Harding, was able to successfully establish the monastery and began attracting some of the most talented and inspired men throughout Europe. It was from this new outpouring of gifted individuals that St. Bernard of Clairvaux was to emerge in 1112.

The inspired teachings of St. Bernard and other Cistercian Fathers added a new dimension to the *Rule of St. Benedict*, and together they provide the very heart, spirit and soul of Cistercian Reform. Where Benedict had written the *Rule*, Bernard and others expounded on it, and through divine intervention they provide an incredible mystical blueprint of the spirituality of Jesus Christ and the soul of mankind.

In 1115, Bernard became abbot of a monastery founded at Clairvaux, France. During this period, Cistercian monasticism began to spread rapidly throughout Europe, and within twenty-five years of Clairvaux's founding, daughter houses of Cîteaux began opening at the rate of ten a year, later increasing to twenty yearly. By 1153, the year of St. Bernard's passing, Cistercian houses numbered 339.

For any community to exist in the world, unless it resorts to begging as some orders have done, there has to be a livelihood that allows it to exist. Monasteries over the course of time have produced various commodities to sustain themselves: altar wine, olive oil, liturgical garments, cheese, jams and jellies, farming products and countless others. And while this was and remains a necessity for the monastic community to survive, it also represented a problem, one that eventually led to the decline of monastic life.

As with any business that begins to grow and expand, more attention and human resources are needed to operate it. The monasteries became so successful at producing their wares that their businesses gradually overshadowed the spiritual life, resulting in monks whose time was spent more in warehouses and in offices than in church. The monks remained poor while the monasteries grew in material wealth. As corporations, monastic enterprises would be viewed as highly successful by contemporary standards. As a contemplative order it became increasingly ineffective in living the *Rule of St. Benedict*.

By the middle of the seventeenth century, other reforms attempted to break away from the Cistercian Order. Most of them reverted to a more austere and strict lifestyle, with some bearing little resemblance to the *Rule of St. Benedict*, while others adhered quite faithfully. The mother house at Cîteaux and the Cistercian General Chapters showed little patience for such reforms, and therefore most of them dissolved within a period of time. A handful did survive, and became known as the Reforms of the Strict Observance. Eight monasteries belonged to this reform by 1618, and the number grew to around sixty by the middle of the century.

It is doubtful that the Strict Observance would have survived into the eighteenth century had it not been for a young nobleman by the name of Armand-Jean le Bouthillier Rancé. Monasteries throughout Europe during this period were often what was called *in commendam*: a situation where royalty of one cut or another laid claim to a monastery. Such situations arose from the abbey land being owned by the royal family, or in many cases, simply because the monastery was in no position to protest the intrusion. At any rate, it wasn't too difficult for a nobleman to install himself as a *commendatory abbot*, or overseer of a monastery, and skim its riches for distribution among friends and family.

Rancé was one such lord, a child prodigy who became abbot of three abbeys by the age of twelve. By his twenty-first birthday in 1647, he'd mastered the arts of fencing and horsemanship, and had acquired both doctor of philosophy and bachelor of theology degrees. He was ordained a priest four years later, and made his vows as a monk in the Strict Observance in 1664.

Although Rancé's spiritual intentions were honest enough, they were wrapped in his personal passions to master whatever he attempted to the extreme. His desire to revive the spirit of Cîteaux through the abbeys under his direction ultimately led him to concentrate his efforts on one dilapidated monastery in Normandy, France, known as La Trappe.

La Trappe was to be Rancé's final conquest. In 1662, he took residence at the old monastery and proceeded to revitalize it, bringing in monks of the Strict Observance. Deciding to join the order, Rancé entered the novitiate where his extremist personality would tolerate nothing less than the most austere of monastic observances, which he brought back from the days of old with much fervor. In 1664, he made his final vows and assumed his role as the abbot in residence of La Trappe.

As abbot, Rancé brought back the austerity that had originally been part of Cistercian monasticism, but in doing so fostered the athletic spirituality that had plagued monasticism from its very inception. "The cloister," stated Rancé, "is a prison in which everybody is held as guilty [before God] whether he has lost his innocence or not."[6] Accordingly, mortifications and penances were the rule, and with an abbot who thrived on challenge, the monks often found themselves in competition against each other and Abbot Rancé. Nonetheless, the overall austerity of La Trappe appealed to those who had become disillusioned with the growing laxity of Cistercian monasticism. There were many conversions as men flocked to the new reform, and other monasteries picked up the cue from La Trappe and went back to a more austere lifestyle. Truly, La Trappe was having a profound influence on monastic observances across the continent. When Rancé died in 1700, there remained a group of Trappist monasteries throughout Europe which upheld the strict lifestyle initiated by Rancé at La Trappe.

La Trappe was a success insofar as it rejuvenated an austere type of monasticism, and it did succeed in establishing an order that was removed from the cycle of decay that had infiltrated the Cistercian houses.

The political climate in France during the latter part of the eighteenth century held Catholicism as a threat to the new revolutionary government. The Catholic Church had become a powerful organization, and its monastic infrastructure throughout Europe represented an imposing influence on French society. The French government passed a law in 1789 that confiscated all property of religious orders, sending priests and monks scattering throughout the countryside as rectories and monasteries were taken over by French soldiers. Many religious were captured or executed as they made their way to the Swiss border. Other more fortunate souls were able to escape and start new foundations away from French soil.

The monks at La Trappe were somewhat better off for the time being. They were allowed to stay with the condition that no new postulants could be taken in. The theory was that the abbey would eventually perish without new blood to carry on. Twenty-six brothers and their novice master, Dom Augustin de Lestrange, decided that this was an unacceptable situation. In April of 1791, they left La Trappe and made their way to the French border. An agreement had been made to begin a new foundation in Switzerland. The trip did not go unnoticed by the French government, which stopped the monks in an attempt to prevent them from leaving. They managed to escape, and settled in an old Carthusian charter house called La Val Sainte.

Life at the new foundation apparently was not easy, and as Merton remarked, "The Cistercian life of the twelfth century was nothing, compared with the privations and difficulties and hardships that were suffered by Dom Augustin and his men."[8]

Back in France, the atheistic government realized that the only way to extinguish Catholicism and monasticism was to remove all those religious who didn't toe the line. To set this trap, another decree was passed in April of 1793, that required all religious to swear allegiance to France or be deported.

The choice was an obvious one for most priests and monks, and a mass exodus ensued that claimed the remaining brothers at La Trappe, who fled the monastery. The majority headed for La Val Sainte, others joined orders where they could, and at least two were executed. Monks from abbeys throughout France were captured and either placed in chain gangs, executed, or died through substandard conditions during their internment. It turned out to be an effective house cleaning by the French government.

The security of La Val Sainte was in serious question as the Revolution swept across France. Dom Augustin began new foundations in Spain and as far away as England, including attempts to settle in Germany, Austria and Poland. But with the turmoil in Europe at this time, Dom Augustin envisioned a safe and peaceful haven across the seas in America.

It was an incredibly difficult and massive undertaking to sail across the ocean and find a suitable settlement in the New World. After two thwarted attempts, a third group of Trappists boarded a vessel at Amsterdam for the trip to Baltimore, Maryland. It was a nightmare, fraught with cramped quarters and a shortage of provisions. After landing and recuperating from the ordeal, the entourage made their way to Louisville, Kentucky, where they settled in 1805. The trip by covered wagons had taken its toll on the little community, for three priests died after reaching Louisville. The foundation lasted only until 1808, when they once again set out for a better location. This time they found themselves in Illinois, having accepted an offer of four hundred acres of land that was soon found to be an Indian burial ground.

In the interim, the fall of Napoleon in France completely transformed the politics of that country, and once again France was made safe for Catholics and the religious. Monasteries were reclaimed, including La Trappe, and suddenly America seemed a less attractive option in light of the struggle to overcome the wilderness and the ever-present language barrier. One final attempt was made to start a foundation in New York, but by 1814 the Trappists were on a ship headed back to France.

Up until this time, the monks who had come to America were observing the usages of La Val Sainte, which itself harked back to Rancé at La Trappe. The exclusion of a contemplative focus in the order was an important omission, and as it stood, the Trappists were not yet formed as the contemplative order for which they've become known.

Dom Augustin, the forceful leader behind the first Trappist American campaign, died in 1827. An abbot by the name of Dom Antoine de Beauregard from a foundation in France called Melleray reevaluated St. Benedict's *Rule*, and reinstated it at the core of the Trappist reform.

By 1847, Melleray was full to capacity, and once again monastic eyes gazed toward America. Dom Antoine sent his prior, Father Paulins, to Kentucky on a search for land. He arrived there in 1847, and purchased a fourteen-hundred acre farm known as Gethsemani. On December 21, 1848, forty-five monks from Melleray founded the Abbey of Gethsemani, the first lasting Cistercian monastery in America.

With the changes made by Dom Antoine in restoring the Trappists to the *Rule of St. Benedict*, there existed three distinct Trappist reforms which followed the usages set forth by Rancé, Dom Augustin and Dom Antoine. The three reforms united in 1892, under the title "Order of the Strict Observance." It has remained so ever since.

Over the years that followed, through good times and bad, the monastery in Gethsemani grew to a point where it had to start new foundations across the United States. In the aftermath of World War II and the Korean War, the influx of new postulants to the monastery greatly increased. Sensing the need for yet another foundation to ease the overpopulation at Gethsemani, in 1953 Abbot James Fox began looking for a suitable location. He focused his sights on a plot of land in Northern California that had been one of the largest and most successful vineyards and wineries in the United States during the late 1800's. The Stanford Ranch was owned and operated by former California Governor Leland Stanford, who also made his name as one of the "Big Four" in constructing the Central Pacific portion of the Transcontinental Railroad.

The vast tract of the original estate had been subdivided into smaller parcels, and Dom James purchased 583 acres of this fertile farm land for Gethsemani's fifth daughter house, Our Lady of New Clairvaux. In July of 1955, twenty-seven monks set out in silence by train to make the cross-country trip to California. It was a far cry from the covered wagons and river barges of journey's past. When these monks from Gethsemani stepped from their sleeping cars at the Southern Pacific Railroad depot in Sacramento, California, and made the brief highway trip to a tiny town called Vina, they were to begin a new adventure filled with cows, walnuts, prunes, and the Holy Spirit at the Abbey of Our Lady of New Clairvaux.

✝   ✝   ✝

Our Daily Bread

. . . the chaos of greed, violence, ambition and lust which the New Testament calls "the World," (I John 2:16) is to a great extent the reign of untruth. It is a place of confusion and falsehood where the spirit is enslaved and where one does not easily learn God's ways.

Thomas Merton

When we look at the monastic life today, it is in such strong contrast from the so-called "real world" in which we live that it's hard for many to understand why a person would want to leave society and physically separate themselves from the mainstream. As one who was once totally ignorant of the deeper implications of prayer, the Holy Spirit, grace and even the true nature of Jesus Christ, I can fully appreciate a skepticism or confusion on the part of those individuals who have difficulty comparing the seemingly concrete realities of daily living with the more ethereal parameters of the monastic vocation. After all, from birth we take our reality pretty much for granted; we accept what is dished out to us.

The answer really depends on whether you choose to take the material world or the spiritual on faith. We're much more comfortable and accustomed to an existence we can define with our five senses. There's a saying about some celebrities, that when they get to a certain point in their careers they begin believing in their own hype; a larger-than-life perception of themselves courtesy of their publicity agent. We all fall prey to believing our own hype, and we take a lot for granted each day when we get out of bed.

I remember sitting in my room at the monastery reading one evening before bed when I looked up from my book and saw everything in the room before me as having at one time been an idea in someone's mind: the bed, the chair, the table, the lamp, etc. And even when I dissected each object into the materials and processes that produced them, they too, had been merely ideas at one time or another; thousands upon thousands of ideas combining to make that bed, chair, table and lamp.

And then if I removed each of these ideas one by one — metal for tools to carve the wood, processes to forge the steel, plastic, textiles, nails, plaster, paint, etc. — every item in the room systematically disappeared until the entire guest house had vanished from existence. Carried further, I continued to remove the ideas of humanity until everything on this planet that is human-made was gone, which left only nature in its original created form.

My experience that night brought home to me how we are truly cocreators with God of our own reality, and how transparent and frail that reality actually is. So if reality itself is merely an illusion — an untruth as Merton so aptly described it — why are we inclined to believe in this untruth and hold skeptical the spiritual realm?

A man who writes the novice master of a Trappist monastery has, on some level, pierced the material illusion and has come to the conclusion that there's got to be more to life than what his five senses tell him. When he enters the monastery, he then begins the process of stripping away this untruth that prevents him from attaining a perfect union with God. It's not that he needs to go to a monastery to locate God, but the monastic life affords the necessary solitude away from the world's hustle, bustle and illusion to begin his inner search.

"The monk becomes a stranger to the world of other men," writes Merton in a Trappist handbook, "not because secular life is evil, but because he travels to a new region of the Spirit 'which God will show him,' to which he is led by divine grace and providence and where he will spend the rest of his days in the presence of God....."

The perception by some that a monk drops out from society and becomes a non-productive member only holds water if one believes that the material world is our *sole* reality, and that prayer is not a valid contribution to humanity.

The model for the Cistercian monastic community came from Jerusalem during the time of the apostles. After the descent of the Holy Spirit upon the apostles and Christ's mother Mary, they all lived together in what is called *communio,* as described in the first chapters of the Acts of the Apostles.

Those who believed shared all things in common; they would sell their property and goods, dividing everything on the basis of each other's need.
Acts 2:44-45

The abbey church, built by the monks after their arrival in 1955. The walkway to the church from the guest houses — on the other side of the fence — is now totally obscured by trees.

"In our spiritual tradition," writes Abbot Thomas X. Davis, in his essay on *Cistercian Communio*, "there exists a dynamic wherein through love, persons enter into immediate contact with one another and, in doing so, undergo an authentic loss of 'self'."[1]

It is this loss of "self" through sharing of physical, psychological and spiritual aspects of the monastery — prayer, meals, work, sacrifice, schedule, etc. — that is a vital, living expression of a monk's charity toward his brothers. The whole idea behind *communio* is that through a *common will* and sharing love within the community, a monk can more readily attain a self-*less* love for his brothers, and experience a oneness through the intercession of the Holy Spirit, who acts as a kind of "spiritual glue" that holds the entire community together. The monk does this by appropriating a mind and behavior proper to one dedicated to Christ by monastic life. He finds himself as an individual "in Christ," not by being self-assertive or self-centered. Christ is at the center of this *communio*; its members being drawn into Him like the spokes on a wheel.

The mystical relationship between the monk and Jesus Christ, which we will look at in more detail in the next chapter, is the ultimate objective of the contemplative life. Union with God, however, is only secondary to the actual process of attainment, or the lifestyle by which a monk perseveres.

Thomas Merton, a Trappist monk for twenty-seven years, outlined several prerequisites for the monk aspiring to the spiritual life:

1) The first step in the monk's ascent to God will be to recognize the truth about himself — and face the fact of his own duplicity. ("Duplicity" is defined in the next chapter.) That means: simplicity in the sense of sincerity, a frank awareness of one's own shortcomings.

2) He will also have to overcome the temptation to excuse himself and argue that he is not, in fact, what he is (whether he argues with others, with himself or with God, it does not matter). Hence, simplicity in the sense of meekness; self-effacement, humility.

3) He must strive to rid himself of everything that is useless, unnecessary to his one big end: the recovery of the Divine Image, and union with God. Now, simplicity takes on the sense of total and uncompromising mortification.

a) Of the lower appetites: hence, the simplicity in food, clothing, dwellings, labor, and manner of life.

b) Of the interior senses and the intellect: This means simplicity in devotions, studies, methods of prayer, etc., and calls for the complete simplification in liturgical matters and decoration of churches for which the early Cistercians were so famous.

c) Of the will: This is the most important task of all. In the works of St.Bernard, the amount of space devoted to other forms of mortification is practically insignificant in comparison to the scores of pages which are given up to the attack on self-will and its utter destruction. Hence the stress on the great Benedictine means of penance, which resumes all others for the monks: obedience. This will produce that simplicity which is synonymous with docility, the trustful obedience of a child towards his father; the supernatural, joyous obedience of the monk who seeks to prove his love for Christ by seeing him in his representative, the abbot. [2]

I cannot help but imagine the varied reactions to Merton's precepts! They are totally opposite from all of the sensibilities and desires by which we function on a daily basis. The fact is, a monk struggles, fails, and succeeds in these areas with the same frailty as any of us.

As one might imagine, coming into the monastery away from the troubles of our world can offer a refreshing change. There often exists what the monks call a "honeymoon period" where the postulant, or new monastic candidate, feels a blissful freedom. Inevitably, there comes the "dark night of the soul," as it is referred to, where he begins to sift through his psyche and explore the regions of his mind and soul, revealing that his true self isn't at all what he perceived it to be. This realization is much like a person who is suddenly stripped down to nothing as a result of a natural disaster such as a tornado, flood or earthquake. The common denominator in such catastrophes is survival, and all human beings caught up in one of these scenarios is forced to focus on their own survival. It's painful and devastating — it's hitting rock bottom — putting the human spirit in touch with itself. Everything else that held value is gone. The parameters that previously shaped lives have vanished, leaving souls hanging in midair with no clue where to begin putting the pieces back together.

During such times, the rich and the poor, the mighty and the meek, are bonded together in the common goal of survival, and each must now depend upon the other for that survival.

This analogy aptly applies to the monastic life as well, and when you get right down to it, our lives hang in midair whether we're cruising down Broadway in a new Porsche or staring at our home that has just been ravaged by a tornado. Without all of our daily hype that we call reality, we are stripped down to the essence of who we really are; everything else is like ornaments hanging on a Christmas tree.

The initial challenge that faces a man entering the Trappist life is what the monks call *conversatio morum; conversion of manners,* or fidelity to monastic life. This conversion of the senses from the material world to the spiritual also encompasses the obligations of poverty and chastity, and it's not simply an exchange of priorities. The Cistercian monks refer to this process as the "taking off" of the *old man* and replacing him with the *new man.* Jesus Christ, through the Incarnation, became for us the "New Man." Such a transformation cannot be willed into existence by sheer thought or determination: The Holy Spirit bestows this grace on those who ask and persevere.

The Dormitory

"In the dormitory, the couches are separated by partitions, and the entrance to each cell is closed by a curtain only; the name of the religious and his number are written above. The couch is composed of a straw mattress stitched through, covered with a serge cloth and laid on boards; a bolster of straw; and one or more blankets, according to need. The only furniture in the cells consists of a crucifix, a holy water stoup, one or two pious pictures, and a few pegs. Nothing can be added without permission."

Prior to building their new quarters with separate rooms, these cubicles served as the monk's living spaces in this 1962 photo.

Dinner

"At the signal of the Superior, each one looks to the right and left, to see if his neighbours are in want of anything, and then unfolds his napkin, part of which he places under his plate; the other part he lets fall upon his habit, or fastens in front of him. If he sees anything is wanting to one of his brethren, he should inform the servant of the refectory as he passes, or else give two knocks on the table to call him. He can ask nothing for himself except bread, water and salt."

Pre-Vatican II Cistercian Usages prescribed two-handled cups, wooden spoons & forks in 1956.

Photos: New Clairvaux Archives

One of the cornerstones of the *Rule of St. Benedict* is *obedience*. Christ's death on the cross is the supreme act of obedience to His Father, and the monk is called upon to follow this example. In his book *The Cistercian Way*, André Louf expresses the importance of obedience in the monastic life:

"To obey is to commit oneself to the state of being a servant as Christ was, and thus to make a total offering of oneself . . . . It implies that we are willing to put our own desires aside, even so far as to prefer another's wishes . . . . It is an intense struggle in which the monk will feel he is expending all his strength and being hampered by his limitations." [3]

The monk expresses obedience to every member of the community through the simple act of serving others; cooperating with his brothers and placing the *common will* before his own.

Another key ingredient toward transforming the soul is *charity*. In the spiritual life, a distinction is made between a love consisting of human emotions as opposed to true Christian *charity*, which is an active dimension of Christ. Through the outpouring of the Holy Spirit, the monk gradually begins to experience the love of Christ — initially through his fellow monks — and eventually to all of humanity. Even so, it is oftentimes just as difficult for a monk to deal with members of his own community as it is for us to coexist with our friends, family and strangers in our lives. That in itself is part of an ongoing purification process where *obedience* and *humility* become the focus for reconciliation.

And when we speak of love, there is certainly none greater than the love Mary has for her son Jesus. Because Jesus *is* the Church, in the truest sense Mary — as His Mother — is the Mother of the Church. It naturally follows that our love for Christ must also include Mary, for she is *inseparable* from Jesus.

Within the *Constitutions and Statutes* of the Cistercian Order, there is a sentence that sums up Mary's role in the Trappist life:

Each community of the Order and all the monks are dedicated to the Blessed Virgin Mary, Mother and Symbol of the Church in the order of faith, love and perfect union with Christ. [4]

Thomas Merton further refines this statement:

. . . the whole new life . . . of our new existence in Christ, is simply the concrete expression of the Incarnation, in our own monastic lives. This means that in practice and in the concrete, we can say that Mary is our

The refectory in 1956.

The refectory today.

very life itself, because the new life was brought into the world by her faith and her love, and is kept alive in the world by her constant mediation and her maternal care for all whom she knows and loves in the Infant Christ.[5]

"It is by faith," writes St. Bernard in his second Christmas sermon, "that she conceived, by faith that she brought forth . . . blessed is she who has believed, for the things the Lord told her have been perfected in her."[6]

The Word of God springs to life for the monk from the pages of the Scriptures with a practice known as *lectio divina*, meaning "divine reading," that is, reading done in such a way that one *listens* to it with the heart. The monk's entire day is centered around this reading of Scripture, either as a community in church or in the privacy of his room.

When a monk reads Scriptures — once he learns to get past his intellect and superficial emotions — the passages truly become the living Word of God, transcending language, exploding into the very heart of the reader where the divine message is received and understood. It isn't a method to be practiced and perfected, and it doesn't automatically happen every time he reads the Bible. When it does occur, a word or passage "will literally jump off the page at you," as Brother Francis describes in his interview. *Lectio divina* becomes for the monk one manner in which God communicates with him on a continual basis.

"The Word of God," writes André Louf, "can create all things anew in the hearer whom it touches. It strikes and it wounds, but it does so to reawaken, to cure, to heal and to restore. It strikes the heart especially, for the heart is its special domain. The heart is the only organ by which a man can hear the Word of God for what it really is — the *Word* of God!"[7]

In the guest rooms at New Clairvaux you'll find a copy of the monastic schedule sitting on every table. Glancing at the hours of prayer, it becomes evident how the Word of God is woven throughout the monk's work day:

3:30	AM	Vigils
6:00	AM	Lauds (7:00 Sunday)
6:25	AM	Mass (10:30 Sunday)
8:50	AM	Terce
12:15	PM	Sext
1:50	PM	None
5:45	PM	Vespers
7:40	PM	Compline (followed by the Great Silence)

It seems altogether appropriate that the monks begin their day as the world ends theirs in the predawn silence. The word *Vigils* comes from a Latin word meaning "watching," and symbolizes the monk on his vigilant spiritual watch during the night in preparation for the coming of Jesus Christ. The sunrise represents Christ as the Light of the World, casting out the darkness. This is perhaps the most tranquil time of the monk's day.

Lauds is chanted around 6:00 A.M. Deriving from the Latin word meaning "praise," *Lauds* announces the new day through the hymns of the monks, who are singing praise to God for the glory of creation and the gift of light, especially Divine Light.

The period between *Vigils* and *Lauds* is given to the monk, and is an especially effective period for *lectio divina*.

Mass and the celebration of the Eucharist follow. On Sunday, the abbey celebrates Mass at 10:30 A.M., which allows the local townspeople to attend, and the church is always full.

The third hour of the day, or *Terce*, is a short prayer period at 8:50 A.M. on weekdays, asking the Holy Spirit to bless the upcoming day. "Roman time divided day and night into twelve hours each," notes Abbot Thomas Davis. "Day began at sunrise, so the third hour coincides more or less with 9:00 A.M. The Holy Spirit came upon the early Church at this hour, the first Pentecost. As Jesus was condemned by Roman authorities in the morning, this hour recalls also the beginning of His walk to Calvary."

Work begins after *Terce*. For the monks at New Clairvaux, it can involve maintenance of the farming equipment at the garage, heavy machinery work out in the prune and walnut orchards, pruning, irrigation, spraying of trees and other miscellaneous orchard details. While those monks engaged in the farming operations are doing their routine, there are all the other occupations you'd expect to find in a small village: the baker, shoemaker, launderer, kitchen and dining room workers, tailor, electrician, painter, librarian, and even a resident potter.

During the prune harvest in August and the walnut harvest which follows about a month later, all the monks lend a hand in the harvesting of prunes and nuts, and the hulling and sorting of walnuts prior to their being trucked to the co-op.

Manual labor is an integral part of the monastic life, as indicated in the Cistercian *Constitutions and Statutes*:

> *Work, especially manual work, has always enjoyed special esteem in the Cistercian tradition since it gives the monks the opportunity of sharing in the divine work of creation and restoration, and of following in the foot-*

The monks in choir.   21

Typical monastic ingenuity, 60's style!

Mechanized shakers replaced poles and baskets!

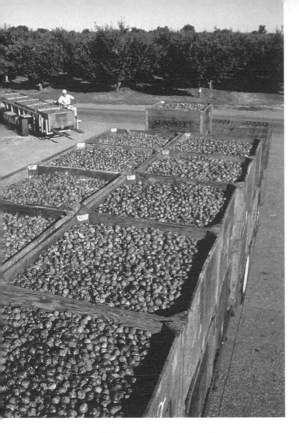

Manual labor is still needed to bin the fruit. A sweaty and dusty job during sweltering August heat.

Bins of plums are trucked to Sunsweet who will dehydrate them into prunes.

"How many monks does it take to repair a shaker?" Apparently, one turning the wrench, two on the ground cheering him on, and another watching the entire operation wearing OSHA-approved head gear!

steps of Jesus Christ. This hard and redeeming work is a means of pro-
viding a livelihood for the brothers and for other people, especially the
poor. It expresses solidarity with all workers. Moreover, work is an occa-
sion for a fruitful asceticism that fosters personal development and matu-
rity. It promotes health of mind and body and contributes greatly to the
unity of the whole community.[8]

Sext, the sixth hour of the day, is also a brief office chanted at 12:15
P.M. to remind the community not to get too caught up in work and
daily lives as to forget God. *Sext* also serves as a break between the morning's work and the main noontime meal in the refectory. The monks eat
together in a large room where the seating is so arranged as to provide a
head table facing a U-shaped row of tables along the walls. During meal-
time one of the monks usually does a reading from a preselected book.
After the meal, the monks are free until *None*, which is a short office at
1:50 prior to resuming the day's work. *None* represents the ninth hour of
the Roman day, and the time that Jesus died on the Cross. This also

Abbot Thomas Davis performs the ritual of purifying the gifts of bread and wine with insense during Mass in the church.

The community encircles the altar during the Consecration of the Mass.

marks the hour that Cornelius received a vision [Acts 10], which led to Peter bringing the Gospel to the Gentiles.

The monks usually end their work day around 4:00, unless the harvest necessitates completing some unfinished business.

The office of *Vespers* at 5:45 P.M. precedes the evening meal, and heralds the return of nightfall. "This experience calls us to a peaceful and quiet reflection on the day," says the abbot, "to a sense of fulfillment in having done God's will. *Vespers* celebrates the lighting of lamps, symbols of lives illuminated by faithfulness to God. *Vespers* and *Lauds* are the two major hours of prayer during the day."

At 7:40 P.M., the final office is *Compline*, which officially begins the Grand Silence until the next morning. At *Compline*, thanks is given for yet another day, and prayer is offered for safe keeping until *Vigils* at sunrise. The Salve Regina is sung at *Compline* to honor the Blessed Virgin, who watches over the monks as only a Mother can!

✝   ✝   ✝

Union With God

If we were to remove union with God from the monastic equation, all of the vows, usages and structures that we've been discussing would be rendered meaningless. Yet, when trying to describe the soul's union with God, it's almost like attempting to build a skyscraper with a hammer and chisel; a handful of paragraphs cannot begin to explain the intricate nuances of such a relationship.

In his book, *Thomas Merton On St. Bernard*, Merton devotes no fewer than five chapters on the subject of this transforming union! It's fairly deep reading for those wishing a detailed description of the mystical state.

For our purposes, there are a few concepts regarding the nature of the soul that we should briefly examine that will add greater clarity to the purpose behind the monastic life. These concepts seriously altered my own perception of God, Jesus Christ and the soul when I first discovered them.

Bernard of Clairvaux wrote extensively about the relationship between God and the soul. Many may recall the Sunday-school definition that human beings are made "in the image and likeness of God." I had always puzzled over the meaning of this statement. What kind of an image does God have, and what's the difference between an image and a likeness?

In his works, Bernard offers different analysis of *image* and *likeness*. In *Grace and Free Will*, the *image* of God in a human being is that person's *free will*. It's one's *potential* for God, which can never be lost.[1] *Likeness* of God is making good use of *free will* by choosing rightly. Our attraction for sin reeks havoc in this area, constantly attempting to pull us away from making right choices in our lives, thus frustrating one's *potential* for God, but again, never destroying it.

In his homilies on *The Song of Songs*, homilies 80 to 82, Bernard presents the Word [Jesus Christ] as the *image* of God. In this schema, *image* for human beings is the share in the Word's dignity and uprightness. This uprightness can be lost by sin. *Likeness* to God for the human being is immortality, free choice and simplicity. These three can never be lost, but sin entraps free choice and covers the soul's simplicity with a *duplicity*, which results in our "false self."[2]

"St. Paul refers to Christ as the *image* of the Unseen God," adds Abbot Thomas Davis. "In other words, He [Jesus Christ] is the God whom we can see. He is God made visible. In His divine nature, Christ posseses all the attributes of the Father; in His human nature He is the only one to materialize perfectly what it means for a human to be such. *Free will* is seen as the *image* of God because that is what makes a human most human: self-determination and being capable of choosing good."

Unfortunately, the false identity, or *duplicity*, of the soul is what most of us have come to know as our real "self," and *that* is the layering that a monk is struggling to remove.

I liken it to a beautiful old Spanish-style house built in the 1920's with the original lathe and sculptured plaster walls intact. During a remodeling, along comes a contractor who thoughtlessly places plasterboard over the original wall. The Spanish plaster still remains hidden under the new layering — it is not destroyed — yet the new owners of the house will only ever see the plasterboard that has been laid over the old.

As with our theoretical plaster walls, the added layering that creates the soul's *duplicity* is merely sin and corruption that our fallen human nature has placed over God's original design. And like the wall, the beauty of the original nature of the soul remains, but lies hidden until somebody pokes through the false layer and discovers what lies beneath.

The *free will* that God bestowed upon us as a gift was left intact, but has become a millstone as well as a freedom. *Free will* simply means that we can chose to do as we wish, and therein lies the rub.

St. Bernard also explains that we are constantly fooled and held fast by our own desires of the flesh, which seeks happiness through material objects as a substitute for the true happiness we lost to Original Sin. As a result, we face a continual battle with the will of God to do good.

Thomas Merton, in his extraordinary work on the writing of St. Bernard, explains:

> *What is meant by an intention to please ourselves? St. Bernard says it is an act of the will moving primarily towards satisfaction of our own desires. The will acts simply because we want this, we like that, we think this is right, we feel like doing such and such a thing. It is not always easy to say when such motives are the ones behind our acts until these desires come in conflict with (a) God's signified will, laws, rules, (b) the will or*

28

desires or interests of others, (c) providential circumstances. If such obstacles destroy our peace of mind, cause us to rebel, to get excited, to lose our tempers, or to become depressed, despondent or finally, to override the will of God and man alike to get our own way, then we have clear evidence that our intention was more or less selfish (in proportion to the disturbance) no matter what fine reasons we may have given for our act beforehand.[3]

We can now see the dilemma that defines our lives, and it becomes increasingly clear that the choices remain the same whether we're within the confines of society or in a monastery. It boils down to *our* will or God's.

As a monk begins to succeed in purging himself of human cravings, his soul advances to a condition where it craves only God, and all else falls terribly short. Yet even in this state, the imprint of *duplicity* remains on the soul like a footprint in the sand. "The new 'form' of divine life," notes Merton, "has begun to live in the soul . . . . But all traces of the old form are not yet expelled by any means. On the contrary, below transforming union the Christian soul will always be a battleground between those two contrary forms."[4]

All human attributes aside, the stage is now set for a more intimate relationship and union with the Word. The imagery of Christ Jesus as the Bridegroom, and the soul as His Spouse, is often used to communicate this intimacy. As the soul of a person progresses through a self-less love of God, this intimacy deepens. A soul can be "visited" by God, as Father Timothy mentions in his interview: "There's an awareness of God, but you can't locate any one of your feelings or anything . . . . That's maybe just one short moment sometimes, and then you're back with your feet on the ground."

A person still functions in all outward appearances as before, with the added dimension of this increased awareness and love for God.

In marriage, two lovers become united as one flesh, and in union with God, the soul is not merely "visited" by God through a relationship, but the soul and God become one and the same through pure love. Love brings about a conversion of the will to God; a conversion quite profound and voluntary. This love orders one's whole life to God. So totally does the soul unite with God that it would be like a wife merging with her husband to the point of being indistinguishable! The soul does not become God, but becomes what God *is*, namely, love. God is love [1John 4:8].

"What happens therefore," says Merton, "is that the divine nature becomes ours; the divine perfections become ours; the life of God becomes our life. His truth, His goodness, His love, His might not only entirely possesses the substance of our souls but overflow into our faculties so that it is God himself that moves them and not we ourselves."[5]

The obvious question left unanswered is, "Does a monk ever really attain such a union?"

"Such experiences aren't talked about," says novice master Father Paul Mark, "because it is more prudent to keep silent. We don't actively seek the experience, for that is vain glory if not outright pride. But we are called to prepare for it. This is why faith is important in our lives, because we don't know if and when union with God will happen, at least to the intense degree that we believe is possible on this earth. The gift is God's, but I am convinced the experience is more common than monks may admit."

✝   ✝   ✝

The Interviews

T he following interviews are presented in an essay form to maintain their flow and to eliminate the need to repeatedly print the same questions. Each interview was recorded on tape — one to two hours in duration — and was transcribed with very little change of syntax or dialect to preserve the intimate nature of the monks' interviews. A generic editing of word usage, slang or sentence structure detracts from an accurate reading of a man's personality. Some topics have been combined for the sake of continuity, but no sentences have been rearranged in such a manner that would alter their meaning.

The majority of the interviews took place in the early part of 1991. Brother Francis went before the mike in the summer of 1998. David Rosenberg's experience regarding his leaving the monastery was recorded in the fall of 1998. Father Anthony was interviewed twice; originally in 1991 and again during the summer of 1998 for additional material.

I began each interview with a standard list of questions, which quickly detoured off on other tangents which I pursued with great interest. This individualized each monk's experience, as we all tend to focus on those facets of our lives that have made the greatest impact. It was amazing how open and intimate these men became once they overcame the unnatural situation of having a microphone placed before them. Due to the fact that I knew most of them personally for many years prior to the interviews, the element of trust was already in place. A monk doesn't too often have the opportunity to express many of the feelings that came out during the course of our conversations. As a result, they soon forgot about the microphone and spoke to me as a friend.

Each monk had the opportunity to read his own interview, and all of them did. This was to ensure that each man's experience, beliefs, and philosophy on the life remained constant between the time they first lent their thoughts to tape in 1991 and the completion of this book. An interesting and humorous sidelight was the astonishment of many of the monks as to how they actually sounded in print! More than a few transcripts came back with "gonnas" and various other slang changed to the Queen's English. After careful conversation with each monk, however, all language was reinstated as originally spoken on the tapes. There was much laughter and little opposition from the monks regarding this aspect of the book.

All chapters were reviewed and approved by novice master Father Paul Mark and Abbot Thomas Davis for faithfulness to the Cistercian life and the doctrine of the Catholic Church. It would have been very easy for the abbot to censor these interviews in order to present a good face to the public. It is to his credit that he allowed each man to freely express his views regarding community life at New Clairvaux. In actuality, very little was removed from any interview and in most cases nothing was taken out.

In the time that has elapsed since I first interviewed these men, we have lost Brother Adam in the summer of 1998. Time does not stand still, even for monks. As the years pass by, we will begin to see the gradual transition from the original group of men that I grew up with to hopefully a new generation of monks who will take New Clairvaux far into the next millennium. For myself and many others who know them, it will definitely not be the same. This book will remain a moment frozen in time to record the thoughts and lives of ten monks who called New Clairvaux "home" during this particular period of monastic history.

✝   ✝   ✝

MONASTIC ENCLOSURE
COMMUNITY MEMBERS ONLY

Brother Adam

Entered Order at Gethsemani - June 18, 1946
Died at New Clairvaux - June 20, 1998

When I first arrived at the monastery, "us kids" were assigned to help out doing whatever the monks felt we could handle. One day it might be watering trees with the abbot, doing some orchard work or even helping can peaches. So in the course of these assignments I gradually began to meet and interact with the different members of the community.

Brother Adam was one of the original founding brothers who journeyed by train from Gethsemani in 1955. Over the years I've known him as the tailor, shoemaker, baker or repairman in charge of the many antique bicycles that the monks still use to get around the grounds. And whenever my friend Joe and I would cross paths with Adam, it was good for at least a fifteen-minute chat! With his Irish brogue and gregarious manner, he was the classic Irish Catholic, and was renowned throughout the monastery as a good man, and definitely what one would affectionately call a "character!"

I guess the one line we always remembered as sort of Adam's catch phrase was, "Be the best!" He was quite interested in what we were doing with our lives, especially our musical endeavors, and his advice was to always strive to be at the top of our game, whatever that may be.

In retrospect, this ongoing advice from Brother Adam is perfectly consistent with what he elaborated on more fully in his interview. It is quite apparent that for him, it was an ongoing struggle to be a success in the monastic life, and he persevered to be that success until the day he died at age ninety-one.

Brother Adam is from the old school, a generation more accustomed to steam locomotive whistles than to jet engines. Yet his insight and advice on life and the spiritual ideal are as relevant today as they were fifty years ago. Adam's frank and heartfelt words are an inspiration to any of us who strive for a more meaningful relationship with God.

The original founding group gets ready to depart the Gethsemani train station in 1955.

W hen they're plannin' on makin' a foundation, the abbot picks a certain amount of people who are goin'. They pick maybe twenty-five or thirty out of the community. At that time [1953] Gethsemani was bulging at the size there. They had made four foundations before, and this [New Clairvaux] was the fifth. One time I went in to speak with the abbot. I knew him pretty well because I'd been workin' in the secular kitchen for about four years, so any time he wanted someone to have some kind of food or somebody come to the gate and they wanted me to make a little lunch up, he'd come down to the kitchen and tell me. We got along real good, you see.

So he told me when I went in to speak with him — when we got all through talkin' about this and that and the other thing — he said, "You think you'd like to go to California, Adam?" I said, "You think maybe I

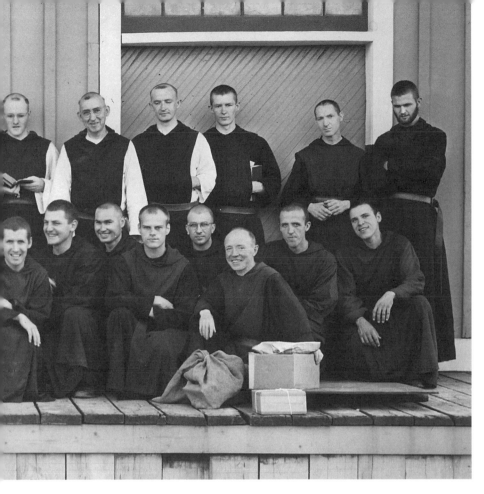

Brother Adam is kneeling in the first row, third from right. Lay brothers during that period wore brown habits, while the choir monks wore the white and black.

might go to California, Father [laughing]?"

"Yeah," he said, "I think you might go to California." I said, "Well, I don't have to give you my answer right away?" He said, "No, it's up to you." So that's how he broke the news to me, but it was about almost a year after that [that we left] because he couldn't get some negotiations completed here. In the meantime, when I talked to him he mentioned, "It's gonna be pretty nice, Adam. We're gonna even fly out there."

I said, "What? I don't wanna fly. I wanna take a train and see all the beauty of the country. It's gonna take us three days goin' by train, and you want us to fly over there in a few hours? No way, Father!"

"Aw," he said, "sure Adam. It'll save time." I said, "Well, you're the only one who wants to save time!" I thought, "Here Adam, this is gonna be a vacation [laughing]!"

It so happened that we couldn't get the planes so we had to go by train, and that was one of the most excitin', enjoyable things I ever had, goin' on that train. Well, we took the train from Gethsemani to Chicago. The local train brought us to Louisville, then we switched on there to a private day coach for us, see, and then we went from Louisville into Chicago in this private car. At Chicago we changed, I think it was, to the Dearborn Station and we got the train to come out West here. We got off at Sacramento, California, and after bein' about eleven years in Gethsemani and never been outside the monastery, you know, all of a sudden, "It's the world I'm steppin' into!"

I come from a big, busy city where there was all kinds of traffic, you know, Detroit, Michigan, in the forties. They had more cars in Detroit than they had in any other city in the world, and buses honkin' and everything, just the regular city noise. And I was quite used to it. It did-n't bother me. It was just my daily course of livin'. But when I hit Chicago and we come out there and we come to Union Station, I think it was, and then we had to go from there to Dearborn Station — we had to take jitney buses and ride from this one station to the other — I never thought that I ever experienced as much confusion in my life as when we stepped out of the station into that! It was just like bedlam to me! Oh, there were buses and streetcars and jitneys, taxicabs, and they're all honkin' and hollerin' and all the noise and confusion and all the shut-tlin' and all that. And we're comin' out there, and for the first time in eleven years I look at this and I thought: "Surely, I never was in that bad scene before!" See? But I imagine that the quiet atmosphere of Gethsemani had certainly changed me, had done something to me because it was a fantastic experience to drive through that city and try to associate it with the traffic and the noise that I knew in Detroit. Then I got in there and I enjoyed every minute of it.

Oh, I could go on and tell you a lot about that travelin' we had. We traveled in our habits, you see, we didn't wear secular clothes at that time. We were just the way we were when we stepped out of Gethsemani. We didn't speak, and when we would be in the dinin' car and that, you know, we'd make signs. It was quite an experience, twenty of us goin' in there to the dinin' car. And a group of women was sittin' over at the table and they were watchin' us for awhile, and I happened to be passin' there and this one said to the other, "Those poor men. They seem to be all deaf and dumb or something [laughing]." I got quite a bang outta that.

So we come to Sacramento and we had hired a bus to take the reli-gious from Sacramento to Vina, and then of course there was several priests there to greet us at Sacramento, and many news reporters takin' a lot of pictures. So for me it was a beautiful thing, and I've never felt a

A few days later, the monks from Gethsemani detrain from their private Pullman cars for the hour bus ride to their new home in Vina. Can you find Adam?

longing to go back to Gethsemani. I guess that's a grace, too.

When we took over here we had a contract with McColl Creamery, and it was a sort of a security deal; we always had that check coming in every month, you see. The prunes were insecure. You didn't know where you were gonna be, you had to get the harvest in. I don't think many of the monks knew much about the orchards. All we had was some apple trees and stuff like that at Gethsemani. This was completely new, and the weather and the irrigation system, that was all new for us. This idea of irrigation ditches going through the property, we never had that at Gethsemani. So yeah, it was a new ball game to come out here, you see?

Oh, it was rough goin'! It was hard. They had, I'd say, maybe one-third of the prune orchards that we've got today, and we also had a dairy herd. We had about a hundred cows here, and they were here when we come, and two bulls. Did you go in and see the pottery? That was the milkin' barn.

Of course, the way the old owners did it, they had a milkin' barn there and milked the cows, and they had seculars do it all, you know, and they would be pushin' and slappin' the cows around and gettin' 'em in there and gettin' 'em out and hollerin' at 'em. When we took over, we'd pat the cow on the head — stroke it a few times, stroke his back — maybe say, "Hi Bossy. I'm gonna milk ya!" or something like that, see. Well, the cow doesn't know what was happenin'! Finally they got used to it.

We had a dairy farm in Gethsemani. I'd say about a hundred cows. Oh yeah. And in my novitiate days the novices were the ones that done the milkin', so I'd be gettin' up three or three-thirty in the morning, see, through the mornin' office. Well, the choir monks, they stayed in there because they have to continue saying their office, and we went out and we milked. I think I had four cows that I milked.

Okay, so we come here and we built the milk up. We started making a lot of changes in the way we handled the cows. The system was, of

"Head 'em up, move 'em out!" Monks turn cowboys with the dairy herd in 1956.

course, we didn't do it by hand then, we had machines, and from the machines the milk went through a stainless steel pipe into a big tank, and then the McColl truck come up there and pumped the milk into that. And the big thing about a dairy herd, you've got rules and regulations you've got to live up to. It got to be a regular hassle. Of course, we were trying to do the best we could but it gradually got to the point where the brothers involved in it were spendin' more time over there taking care of the cows, cleanin' up, milkin' and gettin' the hay in and all kinds of things. You know, they were spendin' most of the time over there when they should be in church. So finally the boss [abbot], he blew the whistle. He said, "No, we have to make some kind of a change with all this. We didn't come here to be cowboys, we came here to be monks, and the way we're going right now we're like a bunch of cowboys." So he

The milking barn.

said we're either going to give up the cows and go into orchards, or get some other means of livelihood because the cows are takin' up too much time and energy.

Well, they kicked that around for about a year or so, and they finally come to the decision, "Yeah, that's gonna be it!" By that time we had the best herd of Holstein cows up here in the upper valley, and we had two of the best bulls. So we were doing fine. Well anyhow, we finally decided to give the cows up in 1963. We had three or four fields out here with alfalfa. Okay, we're givin' up the cows so we didn't need the alfalfa, so we started usin' some of those fields for plantin' more trees.

We know that we've come a long way from the old methods, lookin' at the thing and sayin', "Well, we're poor monks and we're supposed to take the least and the worst of everythin', you know, the poorest equipment should be good enough." No! That's not true today. If you want to run a business like these prune orchards you gotta have good equipment, and you've gotta be able to get those prunes out within a certain amount of time, and they've got to be of certain quality before Sunsweet will accept them, and when we need new equipment we've got to get it. You know, look around — we've got a lot of expensive equipment. Just take those shakers, what we shake our trees with. The first time we used bamboo poles, and you knocked the fruit off the tree, picked it up and put it in boxes and put it on the lowboy trucks. And it took me, I'd say, about twenty minutes to knock the fruit off the tree, pick it up and put it into the box. *Now* the shaker takes, I think about twelve seconds. You see the difference? Twelve seconds!

Our life is so arranged that you've gotta have a certain amount of time for prayer, readin', workin' and just kind of meditatin'. Very few people in the world have that. What we're focusin' on mostly now is community, a family life, brothers workin' together, teamwork. And the only way you're gonna get that is from having a real clear concept of being a member of the community — being a member of a team — and you've gotta play your little part in that, you see, and if you don't play your part you're affectin' the whole team. So that's the way it is. And again, from a spiritual point of view, that is why when a monk comes here to live it's gotta be from that point of view. He should zero in on what his main objective is.

My success, *my* end, *my* destiny: What is it I'm really reachin' out for? Today there's a lot of insecurity in the youth. Today — unless a person's twenty-five years old — there's very little point in tryin' to get him into a life like this because he hasn't got the stability, see. He hasn't come to the point where he knows what he wants to do so how can he know how to live a life like this? That's why your vocations today are with more older, mature men. They know what it is they want and they know that this is a means that they can use to get it. A lot of it depends on the individual and his approach to things and how much he has acquired a knowledge through circumstances and events in his life. That's the way we acquire them.

Now, if he hasn't matured enough in that — if he isn't stable enough, if he's an unstable person who wants to try this and then say, "Oh, I'm a little unsettled in that. I'll try this" — well, they catch on pretty soon that this guy is an unstable person. Unless he squares up enough they'll let him go. But you have to have a real drive and incentive to become a success, just as you are in the world. A spiritual millionaire, if you wanna think of it that way.

Of course, we have young people come in here. Dave [Rosenberg] is a good example, you see? He's got a long way to go but he seems to be on the right track. But only time will tell.

Again, for me it's a question of success. I wanna be a success. What am I gonna do to be that success? Well, when I was a kid I started out . . . . My brother, he was about six years older than me. I'm a kid about twelve years old, and he's coming back home and says, "Hey, let's put the gloves on and I'll show ya kid, how you do it." So he showed me how to stand and such. Eventually I got to where I could start going to the gym, and I thought this was great, and I got the idea, "Okay, I'll be the world's best heavyweight champion." That's what I was shootin' for, and I never weighed more than a hundred and twelve pounds [laughing].

I boxed maybe about three years. That's another thing. I was never serious about it. You know, it was good fun and palsy-walsy, that sort of thing. The guys who are in the fightin' business today, they're kids who've been hungry. They know what it is to miss a meal and to go without, and this is the opportunity that they've got. But even with that you've got to have the same motive: "I wanna be a success. I wanna reach that highest level that can be." That holds true for anything, and it holds true, it seems to me, in the spiritual life, too. How am I gonna do it? By usin' all the means that come my way and use them as a means to bring me to where I want to go. And I can take everything in my life — my vocation as a Trappist monk and the way I do things and the way I think and read and speak — I can take it all and I can use them as a means towards this one end, for me.

It's a question of the individual. We have to live a life strivin' to keep in step with our rules and ways of livin' that people on the outside don't feel compatible with, because to a great extent it's meaningless. But in our way of life, you see, we're lookin' at all that way of life that they have out there, and the way they use up their time and the way *we* do it, and it all depends on what success you want to be.

We dedicated our life as novices to live this life till we die, and not to leave the monastery unless it's necessary. Well I mean, that's a big price to have to pay when you can see the next fifty years ahead of ya. Gosh! But these ways of livin' this kind of life are gradually changin', you see, and their givin' a little more leeway, a little more breathin' space for the monk because this young guy comin' in, he doesn't have the same con-

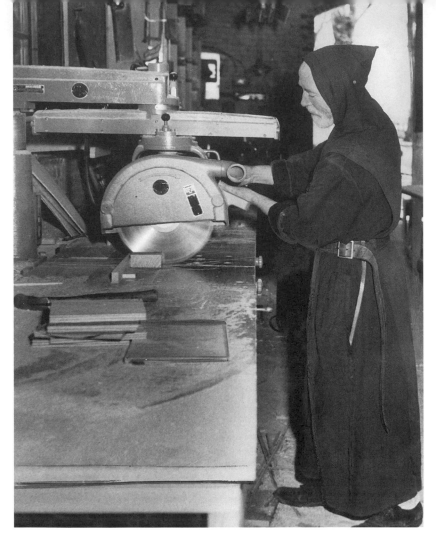

Adam sizing lumber in 1956.

cept as the Order. He's been brought up in a completely different envi‑
ronment, and when you're talkin' about the forties and thirties he'll have
no concept of what life was, goin' to school then and the attitudes that
kids had then. Well, we never had cars. You had to bike your way if you
were lucky to own a bike. Kids can't understand that. A sixteen-year-old
kid today, if he don't have a car, why, there's somethin' wrong [laughing].
Their attitude is completely different. So when they come into the
monastery here they start questionin' us. But now we're back to the point
that they don't *comprehend* the contemplative. They're questionin' this
and questionin' that, see. Whereas, they've got to begin questionin'
themselves: "Why am I feelin' this way? Why am I irritated? Why am I

angry? What's happenin' within me?"

Now, they can do that in a very scholastic sort of way: "Well, I'm just questionin' the logic of livin' the life like this," and it sounds good from a psychological point of view. But you can't live this life that way, by questionin' it. You've got to come in here lookin' for somethin' and this is the place where God will be. You see what I mean? And that's the question of the values, the value of the life and what it's doin' for *me*.

Sometimes I get the gossip, you know, from walkin' in there and I listen to them [novices] speak: "Gee, what's *this* today we're going to have to eat?" I think, "How would you do back at Gethsemani?" or something like that. But, the whole Church has changed. Vatican II came along in the sixties and we made a great change there, and we've changed fantastically since then tryin' to keep in step with all this. And we're still gonna have to keep in step. Yet you get people shakin' their head and sayin', "Well, I wish we'd get back to the good old days when you were silent and you lived a life of prayer and, you know, real monks." Well, what is a real monk? So you've got these changes that are comin' and you've got to be willin' and ready to adapt to the changes as they come.

I've never regretted it, and I've gone through a lot, you know, of uppers and downers. The life isn't a nice, flowin' easy-goin' life; sweetness and all this other. No. You're goin' along there, you rise, you're on top of the world and then [claps his hands] you're down in a depression. You're depressed and things aren't shapin' up, and you don't know what's the matter with you. You can't pray, you don't feel like readin' spiritual books, you're just dried up. Well, this is the beginnin' of the process of your spiritual life, you see, where the old man is bein' dropped off and the new man is beginnin' to take over the life. That was the way in the old days [Biblically speaking], you see, the old Adam and the new Adam, and the old Adam was the Adam who ate the fruit. The new Adam, of course, is Jesus Christ who died on the cross to bring back our life.

It's how you cooperate with grace. I remember my first superior was old Dom Frederic Dunne, and I had to go in and speak with him about once every week or two, and he would give me about fifteen minutes of his time, you know, and he asked me how I was doin' and how I was gettin' along with my work, things like that. After maybe three months and I was gettin' in step with the life, this time I went in there and I said, "You know Father, I start in the morning with the good intentions, all right, and I wind up at night and I've gone through the whole thing just as I did before, and it seems like I'm goin' around in a sentimental circle all the time. I start out here and I go around and I wind up exactly where I was at the beginnin'. I don't see no progress."

He said, "Well, it might seem that way to you. But actually it isn't.

No, you start out and you make the silly little circles and you come back to where you were. But there's this difference: You're a little bit higher than you were previously. What you're doin' is spiraling, and you're goin' a little bit higher and a little bit higher." And I never forgot that day because I thought that was a winner.

What he was tellin' me in those words was what I'm doin' is droppin' the old self in order to acquire and develop the true self, because when you become your really true self, you're God-like, and that's when you reach this kind of union with God. So I always remember what he told me, you see, the spiral, and it was a good point for me because when you get to where you think every day's just a drag — the same, same, same — you go round in circles. If you think of this as a spiral, I'm a step ahead; I'm a little bit higher than I was. Then eventually as the years pass by you get to see where with all your faults and your failures and your sins, you are acquiring grace. And it's not through you! You've been given the opportunity, all you've got to do is acquiesce, go along with it. And it's gonna be that grace that's goin' to make your life a success that God wants it to be.

You can see that it's a journey, and it's gonna be, from my first baby breath until my last dyin' breath. That's it [claps his hands] — the journey! And as I travel out on my journey I begin to meet up with events and circumstances, and these events and circumstances have an effect on me, you see? They're positionin' me and changin' me and shapin' me according to the way I cooperate with 'em and act with 'em, or blockin' and stoppin' 'em, whatever. But they're there, and I have no control over 'em. And it's these events and circumstances in my life that I can either use as a stumblin' block or a stepping stone, accordin' to the way you accept 'em in your daily life, 'cause you know as well as I do, all you have in life is one day. This is it, and when this passes you *might* have another day, but there's no such a thing as a tomorrow or a yesterday. You've got one day and the idea is you're supposed to use it to the best of your ability.

When I deviate too much, I see that I'm droppin' God out of my life, that I'm allowin' this God I'm supposed to be lovin' and want to be united with, that I'm allowin' Him to get out of my life. I'm speakin' about probably little things, but in the spiritual life there's no such a thing, I think, as a little thing. It's a fault, a failure, see? But it's a serious thing because if you continue to commit these little faults or failures, you're goin' to eventually fall into serious sin. And that's it. It's up to you. The grace will be there to help you but you've got to always come back to what it is you want in life. "If I want this I'll have to drop this." Then it's easy. You can become enthused about it. That is why I've lived forty-five years in this life and I've never felt that I've made a mistake.

The monastic version of "Willy & The Poor Boys," with Adam tapping out the beat in May of 1967.

Grace operates within you, and according to the way that grace operates, you gradually become the true self and drop the false self. The problem I think is that we humans are inclined to project all the time: "I'm feelin' lousy. I don't think this should be this way" and "If it wasn't for this guy or that guy things would be much better." All outside; all projected *out there*. The storm is *not* out there!

You see, in this world, it's filled with filth and sin and corruption, wars, and it's a big filthy ocean of vice and sin. And *we're* in it! How can we possibly think that we can get through all that and have none of it wash off on us or get drowned in it? What I've got to be careful of, is don't let any of this turmoil that's out in that world get within me. I saw that so many times out in the world. People that I admire in life. I never could figure it out, only *at the time* I wished I was like that guy: "That guy has really got it, you know, nice, soft easy-going way and seems to have all the right kind of answers for problems." It took me a long time to understand this. What he's got, he's got control over himself and he's got complete peace within his soul.

I don't know if you know much about Eastern methods of meditation. The Christian can also do that. He can sit down in a quiet position, kneel or whatever way that works for him so that he can be completely relaxed. And then he uses some of what the Easterners taught us, you see, to relax and drain your mind of everything until there is a blank. Well, you know that's a difficult thing to do, and then you've gotta start usin' your mantra. What's a mantra for a Christian? Any little few words: Jesus help me. Jesus. Holy Spirit — anything that'll keep bringing you back to what it is you're doin'. And then right down in the center of your soul, enter the garden within you, open that little wicker gate, step in there and you're in union with God. You can't see Him, you can't feel Him but He's there — the peace and quiescence of God in there. And when you come out of that state you shiver, and gradually if you're faithful with that kind of a prayer life you'll become more and more that type of a person, because repetition will do that, right?

You know, when I was goin' into boxing at about fifteen years old and got that big punch ball there, my brother told me what you do is you just hit it, let it come back and then you hit it with the other hand. Let it come back and you hit it again [laughing]. It took me a long time to finally get the rhythm. So that is the way it is with a life like this, and you can miss it! It's the individual, and each of us is different. What the individual must come to — if he's thinkin' on the Christian spiritual life — is he's got to be strivin' at least to become the thing God wants him to be, and you can't be any better than that because that's it!

When I was at Gethsemani, one of the first jobs that I got assigned to when I become a professed was workin' in the secular kitchen. You had a big secular kitchen there. They used to have weekend retreats. Those retreats would be fifty to a hundred people sometimes. They would come Friday and stay 'til Sunday, and they've got to assign a brother to this.

Well, I had never been in a kitchen. I had been with the pigs and the cows and do all the work on the farm and the garden. After New Year's, in Chapter, Father Superior would assign you your job for the year. He went down the line and he come to me at the bottom of the totem pole there, just about the end of it. He says, "Brother Adam in charge of the secular kitchen." Wow [laughing]! I dragged my tail in to see him afterwards and I said, "I can't do it." He said, "You can't do what?" I said, "I can't work in the kitchen. I don't even know how to boil water, Father." He gave me a big smile, he said, "You'll learn!"

So, I went into that kitchen and I had a brother there that was gonna break me in to teach me. He was one of the most beautiful brothers I ever met. We became real close, good friends. He was supposed to be leavin' down there and gettin' another job, so we get together and he gives me the rundown on the rules and regulations. "Okay. Here's how you boil potatoes. How you make good coffee." After two or three weeks,

Some of the best bread ever baked at New Clairvaux!

then finally I begin to catch on. The point here that I wanted to mention is Reverend Father told me, "You'll learn, Adam." You see? And I walked out of his office and walked around the cloister, and on the other end of the cloister there was a statue of our Blessed Mother. I walked up to this statue and I knelt down and I said, "You've gotta help me. I can't do this. I don't know how to boil water and I'm supposed to go in that kitchen and cook. You're the one who's gonna have to teach me." And she did. God uses instruments, and this brother was one of the instruments He used for me.

One day we were workin' there, and we were really busy and things aren't goin' as good as they should go. Yeah, he had fouled up two or three times. We have dinner there at twelve-thirty and it's gotta be on that table, so you've got to make that deadline. Sometimes it's difficult, and when I get under strain and stress I'd start rushin', you see, and I'd pick up a pot or something, maybe it burned my hand and, "Aw, you sonofa . . . . [laughing]"

He would pick up a pot or something and say, "Aw, *Deo gratias!*" A big difference! And I listened to this one morning, and I thought this is something that I've gotta learn. So I told him, "I blow my top and I curse. You handled it very peacefully, and I noticed that you said, 'Deo Gratias.' " And he said, "Well Adam, it's just what we were taught in the novitiate in regards to the faith. You were taught that God wills and permits everything that happens, either in the physical life or the spiritual life. Not a leaf falls from the tree or a blade of grass is grown that God hasn't willed it or permitted it to happen. Therefore, in your life and in my life, when something happens that you didn't foresee and it causes you disturbance, we've got to live by that same faith and see that this is God operatin' in us. *He's* doin' this. Nobody else. Don't project and think it's anything out there. It isn't. It's in you and it's God you're dealin' with, so therefore you thank Him."

I never forgot that day. And you're dealin' with God all the time. These events and circumstances of my daily life are comin' from God. He's directin' it all. Sometimes it's the hardest thing in the world to try to believe that, but it's the truth, and if I can always say my "*Deo gratias,*" comin' from me this is good for me. Psychologically it changes your whole attitude towards it. So I made it a point to learn to do that, and over the years I find it very, very helpful for me to see Jesus in the happenin' of this moment. "Yeah, but it's tearin' my life apart, it's breakin' my heart." Thank Him for it! That's all you can do. You can't change the circumstances.

Brother Adam

You take God out of the picture and I'll pack my little grip and get out of here. And although you've got this beautiful monastery with peace and quiet, and nature all around us, still it wouldn't be fulfilling if you take God out of it. God is, for me, my life. He's gotta be that life. I think that maybe as the changes keep takin' place, more and more there's gonna be a tendency for more men and woman to enter into the contemplative way of life because it's more in step with the eastern form of religious life, where you can have enough time and relaxation to be able to sit quietly and meditate, and be aware of this God within you.

✝   ✝   ✝

Father Timothy

Entered Order at Gethsemani - 1939

During the summer of 1967 I met Father Timothy as he was painting at one of the guest houses. There is an aura of peace and gentleness
surrounding this extremely soft-spoken man that seems only to increase
as the years go by. Even during that first summer when I was introduced
to the monks, I sensed something different about him. His hermitage
shack out in the woods and self-appointed austere lifestyle all lent an air
of mysticism to this Trappist of sixty years.

Father Timothy arrived at New Claivaux from the monastery at
Gethsemani, Kentucky, in February of 1958, and has lived there ever
since. He speaks here about his monastic vocation and the purification
process that we all must go through toward attaining a union with God.

I thought I'd do premed because it was a choice between the priesthood or medicine, and my reason was that in both vocations you
could help a lot of people: that's what I wanted to do. So I guess it was
my freshman year in college I was cuttin' up frogs and all this stuff. I
enjoyed it, and I enjoyed the studies a lot. But one afternoon I went
home and talked to my father and I said, "Would you mind if I shifted
over to theology instead of medicine?" He said no. So that's the way I got
into theology.

Well, I guess the vocation is a mystery. It doesn't happen all at once
— everything led up to that. But I don't know, I think every Catholic
kid at one time or another thinks he ought to be a priest or something,
you know? It just kinda grew over the years. There's respect for the priest,
of course, and then there's quite a few priests who came into my life since
I always went to Catholic schools and college, and you got to know these
priests as pretty wonderful people, especially a few of them that did have

53

an influence on my life.

But like wanting to be a doctor? I don't know where that came from, but I know I wanted to help people. And as I say, a vocation is a mystery. It's each person's mystery and it's a vocation from God, and in His own way He kind of prepares you for what He knows He wants you to do. He doesn't twist your arm, but He sure gets you ready for it!

I got my B.A. in 1931, and the bishop was very kind to me. He gave me a choice where I wanted to go to the seminary. I opted for Louvain in Belgium. See, they have an American college over there that the American bishops maintain. It was connected with the university so that you get those university credits right during your seminary days if you want to. That was a nice gift from the bishop too, 'cause I was in Germany in 1934/35, just when the Nazis were there. I had finished with my years at Louvain and went to Germany and did some work in the academy of liturgy, and there was time for ordination. And the bishop says, "Well, you can be ordained in Germany or you can go back to your class in Louvain. If you come home I'll ordain you in your home parish." What would you do? I went home to be ordained! That was June thirtieth, 1935.

I've always loved the priesthood very much because you know, well, how should I put it? When the priest stands at the altar he is standing there in the Person of Christ, so the priest has that very gift that the Lord chooses to stand at the altar and in His own name to say, "This is My Body." I say that, and look at Him and say, "Lord, *I* didn't say that — it's *Your* Body. *You* must have said those words!" For me, it's such a precious thing, and that is primary to the priest; the offering of Holy Sacrifice. But just being a priest — along with being a monk or no monk — just the priesthood itself is such a precious thing.

After I was ordained to the priesthood, I was assigned to very good parishes. In fact, I'm from Illinois, and Fulton Sheen, he and I were personal friends because he was in the same area that I was, see. He was about ten or twelve years ahead of me. After he had been ordained a priest he was assigned to a certain parish in Peoria, and he had also gone to Louvain. So when I got home they assigned me to the same parish.

I was on a business trip going down into Tennessee, so as I was driving along I thought why not go over and see Gethsemani, you know, it's a famous old monastery. They didn't have those big highways and I had to get on a gravel road to get over to the road that went to Louisville and down to Bardstown into Kentucky. So I went over and talked to the abbot and he says, "Oh sure," I could come back in a week if I wanted to. Just like that! Yeah. It was just Our Lord's grace and blessing that I found myself going to Gethsemani and talking to the abbot there. But it wasn't

Larry VanderVennet [aka Father Timothy with his youngest brother Dan, circa 1935.

a mysterious calling or anything, just a normal thing, you know. I was just driving along. That was in 1939. And then of course, like here, they let you stay for a few days, and I thought I'd like it pretty much and I told the abbot, "Okay!" So I went home and got rid of all my stuff and went down in September 1939, just the time that the war started.

I enjoyed my novitiate, but the thing is, it all depends on your attitude and what you're really looking for when you come to the monastery, you know. I'd been in the priesthood about four or five years so I knew what I wanted, and I knew very well that I'd be giving up the wrong "self." See, we got a good self and a not-so-good self. We all have to give up these images we have of our self and all that. So I just took it for granted.

When we entered Gethsemani in '39 it was very severe, the fasting and the silence. In fact, you gave up your name. My name wasn't Timothy it was Larry. We had to leave stuff. Heck, I used to get a new car every year, and had golf and skiing and all that. Yeah, I had all I wanted, so to drop that was hard for me in those days. It really was a deliberate taking off your old self so that your true self could emerge. And see, people try to fight and hang on to the image they have of themselves, and that's where the fight comes in. Be willing to just drop all that and to be formed into a monk, a servant of God, and forget about your own ego. After all the ego stuff traveling in Europe it was good for me to "hoe the row." Sometimes you felt it, you know, but if you just sit down and think it over, you thought, "Well, it's for my own good."

Our novice master, Father Robert, I loved him very much, and the abbot, Dom Frederic Dunne. You should read his life sometime: *The Less Traveled Road*. He was very strict and austere but he was a very good man. I learned to love him. He was strict and I needed that.

Thomas Merton came along in '41, and there were twelve priests in our novitiate. That was the time when we were getting a lot of candidates. Okay, there I was, having been at the university, with Thomas Merton, Father Anthony of Mepkin, and a lot of these priests who also had degrees. And do you know we had to sit down in the catechism class with the rest of the novices on Sunday? If that doesn't do your ego a good little punch! And we all enjoyed it! It was fun living with Father Louis (aka Thomas Merton) 'cause he had a good sense of humor, and when something happened you'd look over and he'd wink like that, you know [laughing].

When Our Lord invites people in, He is a great pedagogue. He teaches gradually so when he invites 'em into the monastic life he knows that they're not set yet — they'll wham right into the whole thing — so He just invites them, entices them in and gives them a little extra. How about your marriage? You had a honeymoon period, didn't you, and that

56

was real nice. It was real love and everything but it didn't have the quality of the love which you can have after being married fifty years. That's gonna be a deeper love. Just like first of all, a lot of marriages are just biological. Well, that has to be strained out [laughing]. Definitely strained out! You have to go through various strains until there's a really nice selfless love where *you* want to do this and *she* wants to do that, and so you say, "Well, that's a better thing," so you forget your thing and do her thing. And that's what novitiate is. That's what monastic discipline is; gradually learning to forget yourself and think of other people, and then that is purifying. But we all have to go through and purify that. A lot of give and take. What I like to see with old married people, they're just content, you know, no fuss: "Okay pa, if you wanna do it, we'll do it," and that's the way it is for novices. And see, I've been in fifty-nine years. Our Lord had to do a lot of cleaning up and purification on me, like selfishness and wanting my way and all that. Well, Our Lord has His own way of doing that, you know, and the other postulants have to go through the same thing. When you enter a monastery you ask for it, you ask for obedience, you ask for *all* of it. If you don't want it, well, go home! But I knew I asked for it so I had to take it, and sometimes it *was* hard 'cause we're all human persons. It was straw mattresses, and when we came, the one furnace that they had for the whole monastery gave a little puff of heat once in awhile, but they didn't light it until there was frost inside the windows. When I took the novice habit it was January the sixth, thirteen below zero, and in those days when you went in the Chapter to receive the novice habit you put on what clothes you had when you came, see. So the Chapter was assembled and I had to go up to the dormitory. They had dormitories in those days, and in each dormitory cubicle there's a little holy water font where you could take holy water.

So they sent me up to put on my cassock, my priestly robe, and I went into the little space where you pull down the curtain. It's just a cubicle, you know, and I reach over for the holy water and it's a chunk of ice [laughing]! For one minute I says, "Do I want to stay here?" Clunk! "Do I want to go down there and be a novice?" But that was really a challenge for just about a minute, 'cause I knew if I went back home there'd be no frozen holy water. But it *really was cold!*

We had a lot more manual labor in those days, you know. We used to go out and pitch hay and manure and all those kind of jobs. And I really enjoyed it an awful lot. It was formative. And then if you put it in the context of why you're there, just looking at the job, "What am I doing out here pitching manure?" Well, Father Louis would be there, and Father Anthony and the rest of the guys, and we all were just enjoying it, you know. We had to go out and haul in and saw logs with this big

Father Timothy (middle) and Frater Thomas Davis (right) sort through bricks from one of the old brandy barns in 1958. At that time, non-priests were called "Frater," the Latin word for "Brother."

two-man saw for the furnace, and so I look back with deep gratitude to the Lord for my novitiate. It was hard and it was strict but it did something for us. It really did. It was a challenge every day.

I think all of us in the first few years of monastic life, you're always kind of lookin' back to what could have been. And see, I'd organized some youth clubs and oh, you know, hiking with the scouts and all that, so you kinda think back that I could be helping those kids. And there's always that tension at the beginning of vocation but gradually you get into the monastic life and you find out that your reach is much further and more effective as a monk, see. It's like they say, "It's much better to talk to God about man than to talk to man about God."

So I've had the experience of teaching with people, high school kids and all that, but Our Lord gave me, I think, a very special grace of realizing how much more effective my monastic life would be for helping *all*

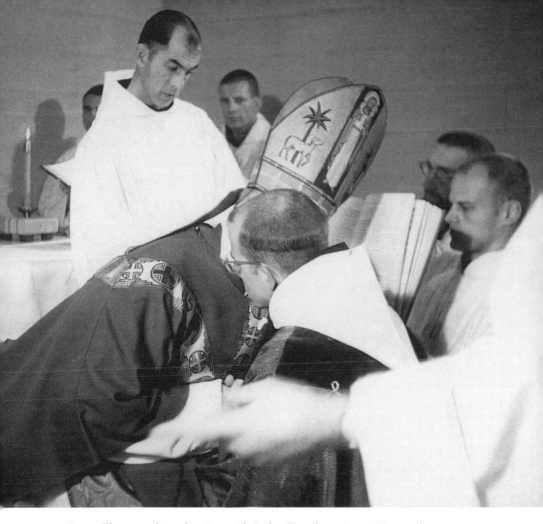

Frater Thomas at his ordination, with Father Timothy acting as Master of Ceremonies on December 20, 1958.

people rather than just living and staying in a parish because our whole day around here . . . . You roll out of bed in the morning and you go to church and the Divine Office and the Mass and all that — all our liturgy all day is the most powerful outreach to the whole world! *You* can do it yourself right in your own bedroom, praying for China, Russia, Kuwait or Iraq or something you choose. You can reach out and your prayer is heard. We just intensify that same thing that you as a Christian can do, see, but we focus our whole life on worshiping God and outreach to the world. So as I say, the time in the beginning you kinda feel like you want to go back and work in the parish, but after just a couple of years you're so caught up in the meaning of monasticism, you know, worship of God and working for the church and for the whole world. I'm very happy about that.

I wish we could get back some of the stuff that we had. Not in the same way, but what I think we've done is when we got into the late fifties and then when Vatican II came along in the sixties, a lot of things were changed. We weren't really serious enough in evaluating the old things before we threw 'em out. We threw too many things out in a hurry, and now they're wishing to get a lot of that back. I would say one thing is silence, and poverty, and different ceremonies; gestures, and things like that that we threw out too much in a hurry. I wish the guys today had more challenges like that. I know other guys here come to me for counseling but I never would compare them to me because I came from my thing and I got the grace and I enjoyed it. It's hard to compare. You just say, "Things are different today," and they are.

I definitely would want to live a more simple type of life. I think it could be more poor and simple like the poor people. We've got a lot of fountains here and all that, you know, and I like the atmosphere just simplicity. And I like *these* rooms [the old, original wooden guest house] much better than the newer. Okay, the new ones are nice and a lot of the guests like it. They accept it, you know: "Holiday Inn. People Pleasin'." But personally, I wish we were real simple, and the reason is that the more nice things you get, the more you get attached to them and it pulls you away from the real reason why you're here, to be attached to God. The little shack I got out there is just a tool shack, and there's nothing there. I got a few pictures of Our Lady and Our Lord I cut out of magazines and just hung on the wall, and a little woodstove, and I made my own table; just real poor and simple, you know. I know a lot of the guys wouldn't go that far but I wish we would be much more simple.

There were discussions on the whole thing. There's just different opinions, different tastes. Some would think we got too much around here, and some think that we've got enough, and so it's a lot of opinions. But what I've learned, see, I've had a lot of the rich things and a lot of the poor things, and after awhile I'm just happy to have what I have, you know. What it all comes down to, very much like in your own life, it's a personal challenge. You could have a million dollars and still live as a simple person. It's a challenge. My sister would buy me the moon if I asked her! We opened our new buildings after they were built, after our fire, and we had an open house. Each monk had to take some people around, show 'em the place, and after I finished the tour one gentleman stood there and he looks at me and he looks around and he said, "You know, you guys got the best of both worlds." I said, "We *have*!" I admitted we have. But that's how some people look at it.

Timothy's hermitage shack.

When God calls you to a contemplative experience He pulls you off into a relationship with Himself, and it's a deep personal relationship way beyond what we can imagine. I can't describe it myself, but there are moments where you're aware of Jesus and He draws you into Himself, and then He takes you with Him to the Father. Yeah! You see, there's no way to the Father but *through* Christ. And then there's some periods that I've gone through for months and months, just as dark as anything, you know. Where is God? Oh yeah, and see, that really purifies you and gets

The official monastic painter.

you used to the idea of living on this higher level. You're not waiting for feelings because in your most intimate relationship with God there's no feelings, just Spirit. You're in awareness. There's an awareness of God but you can't locate any one of your feelings or anything, it's just that. And that's God's gift, and you're just aware of that.

But then you don't stay at that peak. That's maybe just one short moment sometimes and then you're back with your feet on the ground. Sometimes I'll be praying and all at once you're just *so aware* of God's presence: He's my Father and He loves me! Not in so many words but you'll just *know* that. Just a few minutes like that makes it all worthwhile, and then you go out and plant some more tomatoes or something [laughing]. That's my specialty, cherry tomatoes. It's only when you get to heaven that you won't be dragging your old work shoes around, you know.

So what I'm saying, there's different levels that gradually we go through and then you meet Jesus, and in the Spirit He takes you to the Father. And that, I think, is one of the great blessings I've experienced in these later years since I'm getting a little older, that Our Lord draws you into the bosom of the Father. Really! And you'll not only hear, as so many tell you or you read it, but you really experience at a deeper level that God is my Father. Then you feel at home going home to the Father.

It's definitely individual. You have your relations with your wife, and love and intimacy and friendship and all that. Okay, that's on the human dimension. But both of you, you and your wife, there's something beautiful and spiritual about your relationship. It's not biological only. Now, I think marriage is beautiful; it's something sacred and you have, I call it, sex beyond sex. You have the biological — that's a certain relationship, there's a certain intimacy there — but if you and your wife move up a dimension there's a beautiful spiritual dimension that's much richer, isn't there? There's a concern, compassion, care and so forth. That's beautiful. That's a higher dimension.

Now, you can have that with people but there comes a point in your own personality that it doesn't satisfy anymore: you're called to something higher, a divine dimension. Then you have to go there yourself. You and your wife can help each other to get up to those higher dimensions, and that's what marriage is all about, but then *you've* got a call. Your relation with God is *yours*, what God is calling *you* to do.

My experience at the end of all these years is that in Christ I experience God as my own dear Father. I don't put any labels on it, it's just being with God. There's a contentment, a happiness, a fulfillment; gratitude, love, joy, and then what happens is you want to share it with everybody in the whole world, and that's what I do in the shack, I just spill it out to the whole world, see. That's a supreme joy of monastic life and that is where our vocation and yours as a Christian — we're all going to the same place. As a Christian, God is gradually drawing you into that and into His close friendship that He's your Father as well as my Father. Then that joy that we have as children of God, we want to share it with other people.

I think a lot of people in society are going to say, "Come on, there's enough violence and sex and all that around here. Let's cool it, start all over again." People can stand just so much. Don't you think a lot of the young people are sick of it, too? Or are they satisfied? After awhile even drugs don't do it, and very often God lets you go just so long and there's a void, just nausea for all that stuff. And if you look in the Scriptures with the Jewish people, they were His Chosen People, you know. And boy, they'd be real good for awhile and then they'd go and worship some false god: "So all right, if you guys want to go that way, go ahead." And then when they get in all kinds of trouble and everything: "Hey, Yahweh! Where are ya?"

He says, "Here I am! Come on back!"

And I think God's gonna be doing that with our society because it's just really awful. I'd like to personally go out and put a bomb under every TV station! They're just teaching kids how to be violent, and now with the homosexual right on the screen. When TV came in Italy, Pope Pius XII was on the Vatican Radio at the time. He said that we can thank God for the invention of television but it's going to have positive and negative effects because the television can go right on into the heart of the family — right into their living room — and he says there's dangers, very *severe* dangers. And what our society did was corrupt all of our TV. I mean, there are a lot of good programs, you know, documentaries and all that, for which I thank God, but there's a lot of awful stuff, too! So the Pope was right, and that was way back in the fifties that he said that. But I think that somehow or another God will work some kind of a won-der. He can. It's all in His hands.

I hope he preserves our monastic life. The survival of monastic life is gonna be a challenge whatever way, and right now I think we've got a wonderful Abbot General. We've got some wonderful superiors in the Order, top and local, that they are aware of what is happening and they're definitely gonna protect the monastic values. We've got a lot of good guys coming in; these youngsters that do want to come in and do want to stay. A lot of 'em are good guys, and one of the big problems for these youngsters today is commitment. You know, to commit themselves like marriage. Like one guy wrote a book, he says, *Can Anyone Say Forever?* And that's what you have to say for marriage *and* monastic life, you have to be really committed. So definitely it's a challenge for the guys today, but it was for us, too, and it will be for the next generation. But while monastic life is wonderful and I thank God for monastic life, it's not essential to the Church. If monastic life faded out, the Church would keep going, but I hope Our Lord keeps it, at least until I die [laughing].

Father Timothy

It's gonna be sixty-three years that I've been an ordained priest. I passed my eighty-seventh birthday and I'm extremely happy God's so good, and I appreciate our monastic life very much. We're just ordinary people, and I stress that word *ordinary*. I'm just an ordinary guy but God has blessed me with this vocation of just letting go so that He can draw me into His own friendship, and then I'm responsible for sharing with other people the same joy in my prayers. I feel more effective now in my old age than ever!

✝   ✝   ✝

Father Paul Mark

Novice Master
Entered New Clairvaux - 1980

My first recollection of meeting Father Paul Mark was when I was granted permission to photograph and interview the monks in 1991. He was the liason between the monastery and me, scheduling interviews and arranging opportunities so that I could photograph the monks. His dry wit and candid observations about the monastic life forged an instant bond between us, and over the course of the past few years we've become close friends. His help during the writing of this book has been invaluable.

As novice master he is most often the first monk that an aspirant will contact with regard to entering the monastic life at New Clairvaux. As such, he is in a unique and most serious position of responsibility in determining which candidates meet the physical and psychological requirements necessary to live the life.

Father Paul Mark provides us with an in-depth discussion of these requirements and ponders the challenges that faced him and await each man who comes to seek God in the monastic life.

I was living in Minneapolis for two years before I came to New Clairvaux, working at the *Minneapolis Tribune*, the city newspaper, but not in a journalistic position. I was just doing clerical work. Before that I had been in a diocesan seminary program, and I'd completed college with a degree in philosophy humanities.

As a kid I always felt attracted to some type of church ministry. In high school when I read Thomas Merton's *The Waters of Siloe*, it tipped the scales towards the Cistercian monastic vocation. I can't say I really knew too much about the Trappists, and I guess I have to say it's kind of a puzzle exactly how I found out about them [laughing]. But I do know that at the time I read this book by Thomas Merton I didn't know who he was. I still don't know to this day how I even found this book, but it was a history of the Order and I'm attracted to historical subjects.

I can see today with perspective that it was at that time when I read the book, I just felt or knew — although it wasn't clear at the time — that I had received my vocation. And everything after — every decision I made, every choice, every moment — was in some way preparing for that step of eventual entry.

I know what I was looking for in my heart. There's certainly no one earthly word that would ever successfully catch it, that's for sure. Maybe I might say that I was kind of looking for a completion or — I don't like the word fulfillment, 'cause we're not going to be fulfilled in this life — but I kind of like the word *completion*, in that things were uncompleted. I lived a very full life and I certainly enjoyed everything I had done. In fact, in Minneapolis it was at the point where I knew if I didn't respond or enter the monastery I probably never would because so many doors were opening for me — very attractive doors, which can be quite a common experience for a candidate when you get ready to enter the monastery. Suddenly things can work out very well for them in the world. For some, that can be a temptation. I began in some ways to have second thoughts, but I knew to be honest to myself, to be true to God, that the monastery was the place I belong.

Once I got to know about the Trappists then I just started researching and found out where they were. I was in the seminary and Father Thomas [current abbot of New Clairvaux] had taught at the seminary in Fargo in the mid-sixties. He had taken a two-year leave of absence from this place [New Clairvaux]. This place was in very bad shape during the mid-sixties. It was almost ready to close down, at least figuratively. It was a very troubled time for the whole church. There were just so many questions at that time.

So when I was talking to my spiritual director there in Fargo, telling him of my interest, he suggested I write to Vina. So I came out to visit. I personally was not impressed with it, didn't like the place, and wasn't too sure I'd ever want to return! It wasn't that it was a bad place, I just wasn't all that interested in it, and I thought I'd maybe look elsewhere. But I don't know, it was one of those things of the Holy Spirit again, which you really can't explain. And so after I got back, I wrote again and said, "Yeah, I guess I would kind of be interested in continuing discernment with you and checking it out."

I did end up eventually entering, just *knowing* that this was the place that God was calling me to. And again, a vocation in our particular Cistercian way of life is always to a given monastery; it's not to the Order, at least primarily. One is called to a house first, so I would have a voca-

Paul Mark shortly after entering.

tion to this house but not necessarily to any other. And there definitely is a calling, there's no doubt about that! It can't be of human invention. Those who come in, as it were, because of just a mere human compatibility of some sort or another would never persevere. It'd be a very difficult life for them.

I had someone ask me last summer, "How can you justify being in a monastery and being a priest when there's such a need for priests out in the parishes?" It was someone outside the monastery. I said, "Basically, we come down to a vocation. It's a call from God, and if God is calling me, then I *could* say 'no' but I have to say 'yes.' The only justification a vocation needs is that it is a call from God." I don't know whether that person accepted or believed it. I think it went over his head!

I never asked to be novice master or requested it or in any way guessed I would ever be assigned to the job. It was simply by appointment [laughing], like most jobs in the monastery. I'm sure I could of said 'no.' But again, one trusts in providence and your superior's charism, or really, God working through the superior. That was in January 1989.

I was ordained in June 1988. Again, I didn't really choose that. The abbot just asked me if I'd be interested in going on to priesthood, so after we talked about it for four or five months, and after I consented, he presented it to the community. I was quite pleased when nine different people came up to me and mentioned their happiness and being in favor of it. And again, that's the theology of priesthood; the priesthood is always a call that comes forth from the faith community. No priest ever technically decides he's got the vocation, and likewise even a monk. It's God that calls a person to and through a receiving faith community giving that consent, saying, 'Yes.' It could be the parish, the diocese — in this case the monastery — but ultimately, really, the whole Roman Catholic community of believers that gives the consent to a person's vocation.

Ordination is one aspect of a particular monk's vocation. At least that's how I understand and experience it, that I am a monk always and everywhere. But for some reason it's part of God's plan for me in His vocational call that I should also exercise priestly function. If anything, the whole concept of priesthood, especially after Vatican II, is one of service, one of slavery so to speak, and in that sense it's actually far more work for a priest/monk. You preside at the liturgy, homily preparation and you're confessor to the community. Just being a chaplain down in the guest house — even if it doesn't include confession — it's always very challenging, 'cause people do show up with some tremendous problems, and you have to have some ability to at least direct them. In one sense no one can ever answer for another person, everyone has his own answer inside. It's just learning how to help that person bring those answers out within himself. But if a person needs far more professional help, knowing where spiritual direction ends and where professional assistance and help begins can be a very important distinction.

There's a few times I've really been deeply troubled by peoples' confessions. And it's not that a priest takes on peoples' sins, 'cause that's really more God's work. Anything and everything is confessed in the sacrament of reconciliation. But again, it's Christ through that priestly ministry administering to that person, and so the more I forget about myself and empty myself and get rid of my "self" in the process, it becomes less of a burden. But at times, obviously, the human element is gonna come through because I've still got myself stumbling in the way in this process of ministry.

In a year's time I would say we average around eighty-four inquiries. That includes phone calls, letters, people who'll drop in and say, "I want to talk to a vocational director. I want information." And then we have about fifty visits a year, people who come for retreat for vocational purposes, usually with a prior letter. I would say letters have been fairly consistent in the last fifteen years since '77 or '78 when we've really been keeping records, although I could go back in the files to 1955 when we first began. We keep files on everyone who's ever written or contacted us.

New Clairvaux Archives

Assigned to the garage in '83.

The Orchards of Perseverance

The culture today is not conducive for a person to respond as willingly as in the past. In a sense, we always are products of our culture no matter where we're at or what we're doing, so you're in a culture today where there's emphasis on consumerism and the need to buy this or that, and different value systems. That's so contrary to an evangelical life and living with the gospel. Many simply don't hear the call. It's the parable of the sower and the seed again, you know. It's always true: the seed goes out and it's sprouting, but depending on where it's at, it either withers and dries up or the birds get it. But there's always a few seeds that do respond that's gonna produce food.

You have free choice. You can drown that out by all kinds of distractions and other temptations, and that happens in so many cases. I've told a few people to expect temptations between the world, the flesh and the devil when you begin to get close to entering. Sometimes something happens and you never hear from them again [laughing]. We had one guy who was ready for observership and he writes back to me and says, "I've just got a job offer from a movie studio to do animation with computers," being paid I don't know how many dollars an hour. I figured it out: if he would take the job and work an eight-hour day he'd get like eighty to ninety thousand dollars a year! Well, I think he's been swallowed over to the other side of the fence [laughing]! Haven't heard from him in awhile! And it "just happened," you know? I'm not going to force him to enter because again, as God respects a person, so I respect them, too.

Someone who's attracted to our life is going to be someone who tends to be more introverted and more able to turn inwards and be more comfortable with himself, but that doesn't mean everyone is necessarily going to be introverted. But you gotta have the ability to do that because there's just too much silence and solitude. Also, someone who's able to take responsibility for his life. Today there's a lot of structure, and of course the outsider sees that structure. But nonetheless, the structure does not hold the person up anymore like it used to. We used to have a book of usages that gave you detailed instructions for everything throughout the day including how to eat. You had two handles and you had to pick your cup up with two hands, it was that detailed! Today a person's got to take responsibility for his own life in the monastery and make those decisions, even though it may appear that once you enter you just kind of flow along, but you don't.

You can often tell if a person has got a certain maturity or stability in his life if they write to you in an intelligent way with some education. If they don't write enough, especially of their background, usually I have to write them back and invite them to share more of their past. Most often they don't write back a second time. You get used to that eventually

As priest and novice master, Father Paul Mark operates a tree-shaker incognito!

[laughing], and usually the first time it's, "I want information on your monastery. Thank you. Sincerely," you know, that type of thing.

And then there's a few physical aspects. If they give you their age, well, right away you can kind of limit it. Overall, we don't like to take people over forty or under twenty-one or twenty-two. Not that we don't make exceptions, but that's one of our criteria, and it depends on what all they share in their letter, too.

I'll usually meet twice with him for an hour or two each time and talk; find out where he's coming from, what his values are, what his faith history has been like, his family background, get into the areas of sexuality and other areas like alcoholism or drug abuse in the past, deaths — that kind of thing. It's not negative qualities we are concerned with so much as qualities that need maturation and resolution inside. It's more so areas of growth that need to take place. It's not a moral judgment. These candidates we accept today: Are they mature enough to be responsible for their lives? That's one criterion. If a person's not, well then we say, "Become responsible if you can, and come back in a year or two [laughing]." I'm not quite *that* cruel! Overall, most people *are* sincere enough when they come here and when they talk. There are a few who are running from problems.

Some people think when I say "no" that they shouldn't proceed further into our monastic life, that somehow I'm making a moral judgment saying, "He's a bad person." Just because they don't have a vocation here they could have a vocation in other religious communities. But again, I only do that if I *believe* that. Sometimes we get people that other religious groups have just dumped on us. I feel that, anyway. I don't want to do that; I don't wanna suggest that someone should try the Benedictines if I don't think they have a vocation to begin with.

Some of 'em are a little hurt, most of the time they're pretty positive, some of them get a little feisty but as I said earlier, if I think they have some type of vocation I usually direct them elsewhere.

I know when I've suggested to a few people, "I don't think you really have a monastic vocation," they haven't been convinced of that and they've gone to other places and actually proceeded to enter. With the exception of one right now, they've all left, but I guess my batting average is pretty good. Again, is it me? I don't think it is. It's really the Holy Spirit. I need to get out of the picture as much as I can.

But if I feel he looks promising or he looks like he's got things enough together . . . . Because see, that's an important thing in a candidate; he's got to have an integration and be able to do that in a world setting *before* entering, because it's not gonna happen in the monastery. The process will continue and deepen, hopefully, but if he can't do it in the world then he's showing up to escape, and it's going to be a mess for him inside here.

The abbot would prefer not to be involved until toward the end of the discernment when we have interviews. We invite a person here and he's interviewed by three of the monks, and one of them is the abbot. That's standard monastic practice.

So if I'm convinced he looks pretty solid and he's got enough things worked through in his life, then I'll invite him back for an aspirancy, which is a one-to two-week program where you pray with the community. You work in the morning but you stay down in the guest house and have afternoons free for silence and solitude. I'll give special reading and come down several times to do more intensive interviewing. And anywhere along this process I'll say 'no' for one reason or another. If he can't make it in the monastery then I'm just deceiving him to let him go on.

Then I send the person a questionnaire and request five references from him and I contact these five references. The questionnaire is full of all kinds of questions: practical questions, psychological, medical. After the questionnaire has been approved and the references have been received and approved by myself, I invite the person back for formal interviews with the abbot and two former novice directors. Then they interview the guy, and we get together after the interview and sit down and evaluate these candidates. So they're really kind of under an interrogation light all this time [laughing]. Then a final decision is made: Should we invite him back for observership or not? Usually by the time they get to interviews it's a pretty good chance they're going to be accepted because I wouldn't let them go on that far.

I certainly am much stricter in my screening than some past vocational directors. That's not really a criticism, it's just an approach, and I think part of the reason is that as novice director I also gotta live with these guys and work with them in a pretty intense and close level for three years. It can be very difficult where I ask myself, "Am I making a value judgment on a vocation just because I can't stand the guys' guts [laughing], or am I really treating it respectfully as a vocation?" Again, I'm just constantly aware of the Holy Spirit. It's His work, and when I start getting all tangled up in it I always remember that. I say, "Look, God, this is *Your* baby, not mine! You better take care of it."

So let's say they've been accepted for observership. Then they come back for a minimum four-week stay in the monastery, following our schedule while living in the novitiate. After that process is finished then we make a final decision to accept them or not. Unless something serious would show its head during that time that would cause us to question if a person should come back, it's always the person's decision if he wants to come back or not.

They then enter as postulants, and they're in that program for a year. At the end of that year the abbot's council evaluates them and then decides if they should go on to novitiate. That's when they receive the novices' white habit, and there's a ceremony and official prayer that's prayed over them. Then they go under a two-year intensive guided reading program of what we call Church Fathers; the great theologians and mystics of the church [Eastern and Western Church] in the early centuries — St. Augustine, St. Basil — and they spend the first year just reading all these different Church Fathers up to about the tenth or twelfth century.

In the second year they read our Cistercian Fathers like St. Bernard, St. Aelred and so on. Every week they get a new book and are supposed to read it from cover to cover, and then weekly they meet with the abbot for a two-hour sharing and teaching session. So it's pretty intense. After those three years he makes simple profession, he gets the black scapular

Part of the novice master's role is to carefully nurture and instruct postulants during their formation period.

and the leather cincture. Really, the discernment process goes all the way up to solemn profession because the conventional chapter has to vote on these people. They can always vote "no," and there'd be nothing wrong with that.

I feel a postulant should at least be able to get through the first three years if it's been any decent or successful screening process. If they're just coming in and entering and leaving within a month or even within a year, they're not stable enough, so I've been pretty strict about that. I want them to stay around long enough till they really can enter into the life and make an honest judgment.

I'm working with them at a very intimate and confidential level, and

I usually work very closely with the abbot. You find out, or you know things about a person that you can't share with the community unless that person *chooses* to share it with community members. But if he doesn't, then you make a decision and everyone in the community is saying, "Well, what was wrong with him? Why couldn't he stay? Why was this decision made?" But I *can't* say! It's almost like the seal of confession. You really get in a bind, and you trust that God takes care of things.

The novice directors of our American Region of Trappist Monasteries meet every two years for a workshop and pastoral sharing, and that quite often comes up, that type of situation, where you have to make a decision and you can't tell anyone because it's no ones' right to know the facts. It's all confidential, and you're looking like the real bad guy [laughing]. It's not that the community's out to get you, but in a sense it becomes a subtle form of persecution because they don't understand, they're rightfully upset. Some of the more perceptive ones realize that things are going on that they can't know about and they have to just trust your decision.

It happens too, that you get into a triangle: you have the novice, the novice director and a member of the community. The best thing to do in those situations is try to avoid getting caught up in that trap. But it happens. Now there's been some candidates who have been here — fine people — but I don't think they would fit into our Vina community. So in that end of it I'm responsible to the community, and so I've directed a few people elsewhere. It's not always easy to say "no." Sometimes it's painful. But on the other hand, I do really trust I've been given the grace in this particular role at this time to discern with a person. It's not that I have a hot line to the Holy Spirit or I'm infallible in any way, but in conscience I really trust.

There's a lot of reading to be done and a lot of input and teaching from the abbot, which is very, very important in our way of life because the abbot is central to the Rule of St. Benedict. You cannot live the Rule of St. Benedict without an abbot, without the spiritual father and master/disciple relationship which is evangelical as found in the gospel. For anyone who's serious about the spiritual life, one needs an elder, a director, someone who's gone before and can direct that person if we're going to get to any level of depth or response to the Spirit's work in our lives. There's no guarantee that one is going to agree with the spiritual father one hundred percent of the time. That's par for the course to have difficulties with the elder because that's just our human nature. Even a married couple, no matter how much they love one another, there's gonna be tensions there and conflicts that they have to work through. If they work through them, well then their marriage is much more solid, it's much deeper and bound together. I think that's just part of the process that we have to work through. There would be something abnormal about a person who didn't have problems with the elder.

In our monastic Benedictine/Cistercian tradition you don't necessarily have to have the abbot as your spiritual father. But nonetheless, he just always enters into the picture. I mean, you cannot live your monastic life without him but you can have someone else as your spiritual director. That's always understood but there's always gonna be that special uniquely charismatic relationship with the abbot. He is not just simply an administrator of a monastery in a temporal way. And it's not that it's a dictatorship or tyranny or anything like that, or that the community doesn't have its influence, 'cause it does. But nonetheless, the abbot has a very unique role and it's not a power-play role. Some tend to look at it in a sense of the one who has power. But again, it gets back to priesthood, which is about service. I'd never want the job — the responsibility for one thing!

There are going to be those kinds of tensions in a community. I think human nature is prone to slip, but I think the whole process that we move towards — at least here at Vina — is communication, dialogue and the ability to sit down and talk and open up to one another. That's always going to be difficult for any people. Again, it's like a marriage. I've always said this and I've always seen it this way, you know, you're married to the monastery. But when our fallen human nature gets the better of our spiritual ideals and response to God, competition enters in. I wouldn't say there's more here than any other situation. In fact, if anything it could be less.

There's normally no communication between the professed and the novitiate. You don't get to know the professed until once you enter the professed life. Part of the process of novitiate is keeping that separation so novices can learn the value of silence and interiorize those values, to form the novices so they can exercise these values in a more responsible and integrated way once they do enter into the professed world of the monastery.

It will take the rest of the novices' lifetime to find out who these monks are. In one sense we never really do know one another, and you can take it to a real existential level — whether it's in the monastery or in the world — only one can totally or truly read our hearts, and that's God. So in one sense everyone is always going to be lonely. They can try to run away and escape from the loneliness but it's only God that can complete and understand fully what's in our hearts. Most of the time it's a big puzzle.

Lettering in the style of the traditional Cistercian calligraphy.

I'm not too sure how well I know these brothers. There's a lot of communication, and of course there's a lot of non verbal communication, too. I mean, you live with people for so long you just come to know them at a level you never get to know through mere communication, no matter how wonderful the process of dialogue would be or how open you are to communication.

Entering the monastery is like being born all over again, and one needs to learn to crawl and walk and talk and eat in a figurative sense. I was aware right from the beginning when I entered that time is meaningless. Obviously, if there's anyone that lives by the clock it's monks and that bell. It rings and we go [laughing]. More automatic, maybe, than people in the world. But on the other hand, I think we click into what's theologically called . . . . There's two Greek words for time: *chronos*, that's chronological time and the clock. You know, "What time is it?" And then there's *Kairos*, which is the time of Christ. Not historically but Christ's time, the time of eternity. And the monastery is very much in Kairos time, the time of the coming of Christ, in that you become very aware that time is really a man-made thing. What does five o'clock mean, you know? And when you stop to think about that, it's totally meaningless. The monastery clicks into eternity and that eternal, always present, ongoing moment of God. At least that's how I've come to experience our time in the monastery, that it's really already the moment of eternity. Even when this physical body gives up and dies, nothing's changed as far as time except we'll just become more fully aware of the eternal moment that we're already living in. I definitely do become aware of that. It's still *yesterday* that I entered, as far as I'm concerned.

I remember there was a point in my novitiate where I went through a difficult time for about a month, and every night at the end of Compline I was walking to my cell, I was talking to God and I said, "God, I persevered today. I did it another day." I mean, I could not literally imagine more than twenty-four hours ahead. Let's say today's Monday and you'd say, "Wednesday we're going to do this and that." I could not visualize still being in the monastery Wednesday doing that. I was just living literally from one day to the next. It was all I could do to get through those twenty-four hours. I mean, I knew who I was and what was happening but it was certainly a disintegration taking place and a process of getting in touch with my "self." During that time one of my fellow novices said something about solemn profession, and I practically passed out [laughing]!

I remember telling the abbot, and I was expecting him to say, "Look, you've made a mistake." I was expecting him to tell me that I was right, I'd made a mistake and I should leave, 'cause I was *ready* to leave. And then he totally floored me in his response. He said, "Well, those are the things that usually indicate a vocation." I practically dropped dead on the floor from that! And it was because he went through that himself and was the elder who has preceded the disciple. So the elder is kind of the objective presence in this situation, seeing the spiritual path that the disciple's walking. He can see the pitfalls.

I still remember walking to my cell each night thanking God that I had persevered one more day and having no idea when this was going to be over. This disintegration was happening so that I would grow in total faith and trust in God. Because again, if I'm there just simply by my own human abilities I'm gonna fall. So the supernatural, the whole order of grace, all those things enter into the picture. I *needed* to enter into a new level of faith and trust, and it couldn't happen without God pulling everything out from underneath my feet and suddenly realizing that it wasn't me that was keeping me in the monastery, it was purely the grace of God. And I wondered, "What am I doing here?" You know [laughing]? "It doesn't make any sense. Why am I putting up with this process?"

And that's also part of the process. You have to tear everything down to the foundation and rebuild the structure up again, and that's why it's so painful, the novitiate. That's what's happening during the whole time. If it's not happening then we begin to actually get suspicious. If everything is just flowers and candlelight and wine, then you know, "Is this guy serious? Is he really entering into the process of formation?"

You deal more with it the older you get because you're entering at a deeper and deeper level of the "self," you know, the ego, and you're discovering that what you identified as your "self" is really a false self. And then you get at a new level and you realize *this* is the false self also. And the deeper you go . . . . It's like going into a cave: the deeper you go, the darker it gets, the less you can see and the spookier it becomes. In fact, one retired abbot of the Order speaks of the novitiate — of what it is like the first few months or years — he said the novitiate is really a type of insane asylum in that the novice comes to experience a certain insanity in his life. But he can't grow beyond that point until he experiences a certain brokenness. Initially it's very difficult, and a lot cannot cope with that for one reason or another and they leave. It's just too threatening. It's like an alcoholic. I've never been an alcoholic, but I'm familiar enough with that issue to know that until you bottom out you don't seek help. And then when you hit rock bottom — that is, where you hit total brokenness — you're this heap of fragments on the floor. Then you can be pieced together again and be raised up. I mean, it is *very difficult.*

It's always ongoing, that whole process where you're constantly going deeper and deeper in this faith journey. A lot of the time nothing seems to be happening. I find myself caught up in distractions and daydreams and say, "What's the point of all this? Is it doing anything for me? Am I really growing?"

Well, I think mostly it's never really knowing the results in *this* life, because faith really goes beyond any type of results or feelings or experiences. God comes to be in the tractor, or rather you experience your relationship with Him in the tractor in the field or whatever you're doing, or in the person that you're talking with. Your life becomes very Christ-centric. You get connections from all over the place. This is an aspect of the experience of God.

For faith to be faith there's got to be an element of doubt in one's life, and so in one sense I can never really know, and that's what makes the life a challenge and a difficult life at times. I think when we get to heaven — that's where the faith comes in — I believe I'm going to be very much surprised at how much God has done through me for the world because of my faithfulness in my vocation. If I would know in this life it'd probably lead me to pride and prevent me from ever entering heaven because I'd be so proud.

For someone who's planning to enter the Order I would say stay faithful to a life of prayer. Remain faithful to God in a prayer structure that is compatible with your present lifestyle. Because again, if they can't pray in the world, they're not going to be able to pray in the monastery. That would be the thing that's important to me for those who are serious, if you have a serious life of prayer, a serious relationship with God.

✝   ✝   ✝

Brother Francis

Entered New Clairvaux - 1970

When New Clairvaux announced a number of years ago that couples could come together for a retreat at the monastery, my wife and I packed a suitcase along with our shaggy dog, Arthur, and headed for Vina. Now, normally guests do not bring animals with them on retreats, but we had just gotten Arthur and couldn't leave him alone at home. The guest master at the time was Brother Francis, and he couldn't have been more accommodating to the three of us.

His was not among the original interviews conducted in 1991. We got together in the summer of '98 almost as an afterthought while I was in the midst of this project, and it was fortunate that we did.

Brother Francis's narrative describes an all-too-familiar storyline for many of us who fill our lives with so much worldy noise that we leave little or no time to look inward at ourselves. And in the process of neglecting to nuture our interior life, we often come to take our faith for granted. Brother Francis tells the extraordinary story of how God called him to the monastic life and what was revealed after he got there.

Our whole family was Catholic, and I was raised in Catholic schools. I was in the third grade when my vocation started. We went on a trip to the Orient in 1950. I don't remember much of Hawaii nor the Philippines, but in those days you could still get into Shanghai, China, and while we saw a lot of nice places in China, my parents were very wise and we saw some poverty stricken places. I saw that people didn't have enough food or clothing, and I was a very impressionable child. Then when we got to Japan, although it was five years after the war, you could still see that Japan had been in a pretty bad war. A lot of things weren't built up yet. For example, in Kobe Bay you could see ships sticking out of the water, they'd been sunk. You could see buildings had been bombed. So when I got back from that trip, I just started going to

Mass every day. I just *had* to go. If you would of asked me why, I would-n't have known why.

I went to an Augustinian high school, Villanova Prep School in Ojai, California. Some of my friends had gone there and I wanted to go, too. The Augustinians are a teaching order in the Church. They have parish-es, high schools, colleges, universities, and when you entered the school they asked you what you were interested in and I just put one word: sem-inary. So I naturally became an Augustinian. It was that simple. Had I gone to a Franciscan school I would have been a Franciscan.

At first I wanted to be a priest, but then I had a lot of trouble in stud-ies in school so we decided maybe the brotherhood would be better, and I went back east for four years. I spent three years at Staten Island and one year in New Hamburg, which was the novitiate year. See, my par-ents were from New York so I had as many relatives in New York as I did in California.

In high school, I first heard about the Trappists when I read a book by Thomas Merton, and I read their schedule. There was no way I was gonna be a Trappist because Trappists get up early, and I didn't like that idea since I tend to be a night person. So there was really no thought of ever being a Trappist.

After spending three years at Staten Island I went up to the novitiate, which is on the Hudson River, fifteen miles above West Point on the opposite side of the river: beautiful, picturesque country, and it was two days before Christmas. And I remember the snow! Californians love snow, until they have to shovel it [laughing]. There were these outdoor stations of the cross along this long driveway, a very contemplative driveway, and the thought came to me, "Someday you're going to be a monk."

Now, at the time I didn't know where the thought came from, and well, it was hilarious. I just started laughing 'cause there was no way. I wasn't interested in that at all. So that was 1963, and in those days even your active orders were pretty strict. For example, on the second floor there was no speaking allowed where the rooms were, and that year was a very beneficial year. In the morning we studied spirituality, then in the afternoon we had intermurals. At the end of the year I took my simple vows, my first vows. And we were driving back down that long driveway just a day before Christmas, and again the thought came to me, "Some day *you will* be a monk!" Then I realized it was from Our Lord, that He was speaking in me.

Well, as I said before, I wasn't too interested, and even though I had this locution, I *still* wasn't interested. And I kind of said to the Lord, "If *You* want me to be a monk, okay I will, but *You're* gonna have to take care of all the details — *You* take care of it, I'll be a monk." So I still wasn't too convinced of the idea but I was willing to go along with Him.

Then I was stationed at St. Augustine High School in San Diego for three years, where I worked in the discipline department as the absentee clerk. I helped a lot of people, and started coaching grammar school football, basketball and baseball. In 1966 I took my solemn vows with the Augustinians, my final vows, and I remember lying prostrate before the altar thinking I'm never going to remain an Augustinian. I told a priest that afterwards and he said, "Well what did you take vows for?" I said, "God's calling me here too," which He was.

I was at St. Augustine's for three years, and then I was stationed at Central Catholic High School in Modesto, California. It's not an Augustinian school but we were staffing along with the Holy Cross Sisters, and there I became the librarian and athletic director. In nineteen . . . . Let's see, the years are hard to remember! Oh, in 1968 there were some Augustinians visiting from the Midwest. It was during the summertime and they said, "We're gonna take a ride. Do you wanna come?"

I said, "Sure! Where are you going?" And they said, "Vina."

"Vina?" I'd never heard of that. "Where's Vina?"

They said, "There's a Trappist monastery there."

Well, my ears kind of perked up and I said, "That sounds interesting." So we came up here, and in those days it wasn't the same as it is now. There was kind of a dilapidated fence, and weeds all over the place, and you didn't have a nice manicured place like you have now. So I remember thinking, driving through that gate, "What a dump! If You want me to be a monk it's not gonna be here [laughing]." That's actually what I thought! So that was that. I never gave it another thought. Besides, I had plenty to do.

The following year, around June of 1969, it was Sunday morning and all the priests were out saying Mass, and the phone kept ringing. Well naturally, having been absentee clerk, I hate telephones, so I said, "I have to get away from this phone." I went out on the baseball field. I was sitting under the shade of the backstop and I had my breviary with me, and all of a sudden that inner voice came again, "Now is the time," and I said, "Okay!"

I went in and told my prior, who thought I was crazy because I was very active. He said, "Okay, I'll write a letter of recommendation but you'll have to get permission from the provincial." So I saw the provincial and he gave me the whole summer off. The first six weeks of the summer I went down to San Diego and saw my friends [laughing], kind of partied down there for awhile and then I came here to New Clairvaux.

Looking like he's ready to climb into the cockpit of a WW II fighter, Brother Francis is ready for dusty orchard duty in 1971.

They had just gone off the silence and they weren't even speaking in complete sentences. They would speak like a sign language, and they still had the old building; the old Trappist way of the little cubicles instead of the separate rooms.

I entered New Clairvaux in 1970. It was just the closest place. I mean, I know some monks have gone to other monasteries and looked at 'em, but that just never occurred to me.

I didn't experience this a lot but there was a kind of what they call *infantilism* in the order; everything was spelled out for you. And I think in the Church in general before Vatican II, *everything* was spelled out for you: you do that, you don't do that, etc. etc. After Vatican II it was just the opposite. God seemed to be saying to us, "I want *you* to discover who I am, I want *you* to discover My love for you." So everything became more interpretive. It wasn't as cut and dry as it was before and that's a pretty big change. There was nothing wrong with the way things were before Vatican II, but now the Spirit has seemingly led us another way, now you have more responsibility that's on your shoulders which allows for a greater freedom. I was joking but I don't think it's so joking that God called me to be an Augustinian *first*, because I don't know if I would have made it here before Vatican II [laughing]! I had to mature a little more before I came here, and I think that's maybe one reason he called me to another order first.

I don't know that God *chooses* us for a calling; I mean, I guess in reality He does, but He *invites* us. We can say "yes" or "no." It's a discovery. People are here and they discover they're called. Some people discover they're not called. Be open to the Spirit. Surprises are fun but they're not gonna be fun unless you're open to the Spirit. Some of them are maybe threatening surprises — that's part of it — but a lot of them too, are fun surprises!

I think that question is answered in St. Therese's autobiography, the first chapter of *The Story of A Soul*, when she asks the same question herself. She quotes St. Paul. It's a matter of God's mercy, not our choosing; His mercy and His love. It's all a gift, and that's one beautiful thing about the *Rule of St. Benedict*, that Benedict says we go to God by using the gifts God has given each of us. So every person has a gift.

The novice master here was Father Paul Jerome. He was very good 'cause he's the one that began the program of reading the Church Fathers, and we were the first group to do it. In those days — this was just when Cistercian Publications was beginning — we didn't have a lot of translations that we have today so we read bits and pieces of books rather than whole books. Sometimes we read whole books if we had them but usually we didn't. We had the workshop, as it was called, and every Monday, Wednesday and Friday from two to four we read between ninety and a hundred and thirty pages every other day, so we had a tremendous background in patrology, reading many authors right up to the present century. That's why I always tell the novices today, "Be faithful to your reading. Get as much background as you can 'cause it's worth it."

I had eleven years of religious life when I got here so I loved the novitiate. Now, when I first came I certainly went through a honeymoon period, and I started having dreams and remembering things that for all practical purposes I had forgotten; nice things from my childhood. It was wonderful! It really wasn't until I was here five years in 1975 when that intense period began.

In my life I've had a lot of trouble with anger, and I would be out there on a tractor mowing grass just yelling and screaming, literally, at God. I didn't have time to deal with all this anger as an Augustinian, and it took five years before the honeymoon period was really over here. Then I started facing my anger and I got really to the point in 1975 when I didn't believe in God anymore because I had taken my faith for granted all my life. I saw a lot of darkness. I saw a lot of sin in the world and myself. I never questioned my faith before I got here. I mean, I was helping other people who were questioning *their* faith, but I never had time to question my own. The faith I had before was a sincere faith but it was naive. The faith I have now is an informed faith. As a matter of fact, sometimes I don't even use the word *faith* anymore 'cause I *know*, and that's coming a long way. But to get there you go through hell and high water! The truth will set you free but looking at yourself is pretty scary.

And then when I got here, for the first time in my life I had *time* to question it. Time is a big factor. Sometimes I don't even know what day it is, it's all one, it flows. When you're in God's time it just all blends into one. I mean, most people when they're in their eighties or nineties or when they get to the point when they're immobile have a lot of time on their hands. We have that much time as soon as we walk in the gate, so you start looking at yourself. And of course the first thing that you see is everybody else, all *their* faults, 'cause you don't want to see your own. Then you start seeing your own and that's when the fun begins. It was pretty intense. It shook everything. Of course, the tractor was the best therapy in the world without me knowing it [laughing].

So in that same year I started dealing with it. I went to therapy. I started believing again. The first therapy was intense. As a matter of fact I don't know how I never got in a car accident, 'cause I'd be so angry I'd be crying and I'd be in a rage sometimes. I had all this anger at God, my parents, my teachers, and myself — at anybody. I wasn't choosy [laughing]. I was angry at God for all the negativity in my past life, and any time anything went wrong I'd want to walk out the gate. I never actually walked out. I walked out in my mind a lot but never physically [laughing].

I remember one time I was actually in a quiet rage, literally in a rage! And I remember afterwards I went to Father Paul Jerome and I told him, and he said, "What did you do?" I said, "Oh, I just went to church!" And I didn't see the humor of it until he started laughing. He said, "Well, at least you went to the right place [laughing]." I will never forget that.

Oh gosh, the other monks were so patient. This community is really tolerant, and just by their tolerance they helped me 'cause I would get depressed. I know one monk said when I get depressed it affected him. You know, it takes a lot of love to tell you something like that.

Francis and Father Harold looking over a piece of machinery.

I think that anger is one of the practical results of original sin. It's part of the form that we're not perfect, and of course nobody likes to be imperfect — not even us — and when you find out you're not perfect it's challenging to say the least. Then if you're a person like me who had very high expectations of yourself and everybody else, then it's worse. Reality has changed in the sense that as I saw my own problems and my own anger and frustration, I realized everybody else has the same frustration, too. Where before, although intellectually I was helping people as an Augustinian, I really didn't have the experience myself.

And so with all the negativity that I had and all the anger and the total lack of confidence I had in myself, God had to work with me like that. That's the only thing He could have done to call me here. As I say, I never really started having the doubts until I was here five years, so God works with us the way we need to be worked with. With me, all I ever did was say "yes." I mean, God did all the work, I didn't do anything. It's like He handed it to me on a silver platter. He said, "Here!" I had no doubts when I came. If you think about my story, most of the monks here, I'm sure, had a thousand and one doubts *before* they got to the gate. I never had that. I *knew*, I literally knew! And even on the day on which I came here my body was in kind of a — I don't know how to describe it — a kind of a physical ecstasy. I knew I was coming home, I knew this was it.

Very early on I remember talking to Father Timothy, as wise as he is, and he said, "If you come to stay, you'll stay. If you come to try it out, you'll never make it." Well, I didn't come to try it out, I came to stay, and yeah, I thought about going to other communities plenty of times. That was one of the things I decided in 1975, maybe I'll go to another community. Of course, the grass is always greener on the other side of the fence. And I remember Father Timothy saying too, "By the inch it's a cinch. By the mile, it's a trial." And he's right. You work one day at a time, and God does it. All we say is "yes," which we do kicking and screaming all the way, of course.

I've realized by God's grace and by the community's patience that I've grown a lot, but I also realize I have a long way to go. I'm really just beginning, I'm really just scratching the surface and that's okay, as long as we keep saying "yes." It seems like we go two steps forward and one step backward. We have our good days and our bad days. But reading Julian of Norwich — she's my favorite mystic and she is based totally on the Cistercians — she says we have to get used to that. Sometimes we're up and sometimes we're down. It's like a bend in the river. She says first she experienced total serenity and total peace, and then she was just down in the dumps; one and then the other perhaps twenty times. And

Driving a shaker requires a certain degree of skill and dexterity. Brother Joe Gilbert assists "on the ground" as Francis carefully positions the machine under a plum tree.

she says she didn't experience the ecstasy and the good times because of anything *she did*, because she wasn't deserving of all that consolation. Then she says she didn't *sin* to experience the bad times, either, that God lets us experience all these things to keep us pining and desiring Him. She has a beautiful way to put things.

Certainly people get mad at God, but God's not the one who makes bombs. I mean, if we used all the money we use for defense purposes, how many mouths could we feed? Man is down, or I'm down, because I make a decision which is not a good decision. So if I'm down it's because I'm choosing to be down.

If you want to take the Platonic way, man is a compound being, we're a body/spirit, so if you have nothing to do with your spiritual side that's obviously self-alienation. *Of course* you're not going to experience integration because you're denying a part of yourself. People today tend to say, "My life I lead with other people is one thing and then my spiritual life sits over there somewhere, it's something else." Well, that's not togetherness. No wonder people are so frustrated! They lead a good life, they have a nice car, nice family — they have everything they need — and yet they're not happy. Well obviously they're not happy because they don't have the spiritual. It's obvious to me. It's everything *but* obvious to them.

I was talking to a priest about that one time many years ago and I said, "It's too bad that some people don't discover God until it's time for their death." And his response was that maybe in God's eyes that's time enough for them, that they *do* experience it. You know, look at all the guys that had to go to Viet Nam. They say you experience God in a fox-hole when you get scared. Or I can remember in 1960 when I was a seminarian; remember the Cuban Missile Crisis? People were coming into church and you could just tell they hadn't been to church in years and they were scared to death. Well, fear drives people to God and then things become nice, no more wars. So things are nice and they're free and anything goes, then they're going in the opposite direction 'cause nothing is forcing them to look at God. But wouldn't it be nice if they didn't need to be forced to look at God but they said, "Oh yes, God is part of my life. A big part."

I think God doesn't communicate with me or with other people just one way. I think God communicates in many ways. And one of the ways which is quite delightful is when you're chanting the psalms. And although you've chanted that psalm . . . . Well how many times have I chanted the psalms in twenty-eight years being here? You know, you've done the same psalms thousands of times. And yet, sometimes one of the psalms or parts of the psalm will literally jump off the page at you. Literally jump off! And you see something you've never seen before in that psalm about God speaking there. That's one way God speaks.

God speaks through my brothers, through the scenery — the colors and beautiful trees we have — and through the people I deal with doing the groups. God speaks in one big way in our *lectio divina*: the Scriptures. As I said, I was an Augustinian eleven years and I was here five years, and it was after sixteen years of religious life that the Scripture kind of just exploded. Then I knew *He* was my food. The early fathers of the Church don't make any distinction between receiving Christ in the Eucharist or receiving Christ in the Scripture. I think it's Saint Jerome that says, "Reading the Scripture is like the eating of the Pascal Lamb." So God speaks very loudly in the Scriptures. He speaks very loudly in the *Rule of St. Benedict*: "The Cistercian Order is an Order wholly ordered to contemplation." God speaks in contemplation, in our prayer. Sometimes it's a sudden insight, other times it's a gradual thing.

I know many times I'll be sitting, just kind of searching the Scriptures, and I'm usually thematically going from one cross reference to another. And I'll be doing that for fifteen or twenty minutes, and all of a sudden I have to stop 'cause I know God is here. It's just very powerful, and yet it's very gentle at the same time. It's wonderful [laughing].

Remember the gospel where the disciples are on their way to Emmaus? (Luke 24:13-35) Jesus is with them and they don't recognize Him as Christ. It's after He's risen. And remember they said they were expecting this warlike messiah to free them from the Romans? And Jesus says, "Oh you of little faith," and then He starts explaining the Scriptures to them about Himself. Then they get to where they were going and they recognize Him in the breaking of the bread. What happens next is very interesting, and if you think about it, it does not make sense. They say, "Weren't our hearts burning when He explained the Scriptures to us?" But the Scripture *just said* they recognized Him in the breaking of the bread. Why didn't they say, "Weren't our hearts burning when we recognized Him in the breaking of the bread?" It doesn't make sense, but the insight I got while reading that Scripture was — the question came to me — "Would they have recognized Christ had He *not* explained the Scriptures to them?" And there's the perfect example in the gospel of Luke of *lectio divina*. God is doing *lectio divina* with them! He's showing, "Here it is in the Scripture. Here it is in Isaiah, the Suffering Servant. Here I am! Can't you see Me?" And He explained all of the Scriptures about Himself. But had He not done that, would they have recognized Him in the breaking of the bread? Who knows?

Having been dealing with the groups now for twenty-three years — being the PR man of the monastery — the first thing I have to do in dealing with a group of people is tell a lot of jokes and be very funny because people put us on pedestals. And before I can talk about Christ and the love that Christ has for them, I have to first convince them that I'm a human being, and humor is the best way to do it. So I think the first misconception people have about these mysterious figures called monks is that they're some kind of superhuman. I would like people to see us as human beings just like them. We have our troubles, we've had our ups and downs just like they do. Because if people don't see us as human beings, then what's this idealistic picture of us gonna do for them? Nothing.

The monastic life is really a love affair between God and us and our brothers. It's never God and *me*, it's always God and *us*. I find myself praying for the whole world much of the time, for world problems. I have to! I saw China and Japan in 1950, and they were in a pretty bad state. And that's where it all began. St. Therese died when she was twenty-four, and yet she's the co-patroness of the missions. She never went on a mission! She wasn't in a missionary order but she *prayed* for the missions. Does Jesus talk about monks in the New Testament? No, but in the gospel of

As "publicity man" of the monastery, Francis entertains a group visiting for the afternoon.

Luke, eight or nine times he mentions, "Jesus spends the night in prayer." *That's* the monk! That's our life. That's our contribution to the world.

And it's no cop-out when you have to face yourself. Sometimes I ask people how many hours do you watch television, and then ask yourself how many hours do you pray a week, and compare the answers. Who's copping out? I say, "Oh no, it's *your* life that's a cop-out" [laughing] because what happened when I came here? I had to face myself for the first time in my life. I was so busy *before*, I couldn't do that. I'm not saying that what I was doing before *was* a cop-out, but for all practical purposes I didn't have time to face myself.

One of the things that I've noticed is that whether people come to stay for a few hours, a few days on retreat, or as a long-term guest, or whether they actually enter the monastery and stay for a few years and then leave, something happens. Sometimes I can even see it in people, something happens to them. God works! And of course, people come in here and the first thing they say is, "Oh how peaceful it is." What they're experiencing is God's presence, which is always within them but they have to be in a quiet place to discover that presence.

Many monastic authors talk about the cloister of the heart, that you take God's presence with you wherever you are. Saint Peter says, "Stay calm so you can pray." Well, you can get impatient in the monastery and you can get impatient outside the monastery, but God's presence is everywhere. Jesus even said that: "I am with you all days until the end of the world," and "Where two or three are gathered together in My name there I am in the midst of them." He didn't say "in a monastery" or "out of a monastery." He didn't specify where. Even the name Emmanuel means "God with Us."

Of course, it's those darkest periods that we've spoken about where you don't see God. But then that's why the experience is so powerful, because when you're in darkness and all of a sudden the room lights up, then you see God! You have to experience the darkness sometimes to see the light, and they work back and forth in conjunction with one another. Julian says that God is courteous. She uses that word to describe Him, that God loves us so much He doesn't force His love on us. He lets us discover His love, because you really can't force love on a person. The way God works is wonderful. I never saw this years ago when I came here. I didn't see any of this. I'm just beginning to see Him now through other people, through bits of revelation, maybe things you don't want to face and then you say, "Oh, wait a minute. God's here, too." It's just wonderful.

The apostles had trouble seeing Christ as God. They saw Him as a human being; they lived with Him. But if you think about it, today it's just the opposite. We have no trouble seeing Christ as God but we have trouble seeing Christ as a human being. I see all people in God now, but it's taken a long time to see that, and certainly to see that not only does one have to confront one's self, but one has to let other people confront you. In other words, you have to stop judging people. I had to give up the expectations I had of people. St. Bernard describes the whole process in one of his works, *The Degrees of Truth*.

The first degree of truth is knowledge of the self, but the thing that happens is you begin to think you're the only one in the boat. Then gradually you see, "Hey, I'm not the only one in the boat; everybody else is in the boat with me." And St. Bernard says the first thing we realize is that we're miserable. Then we realize everybody else is miserable. He says this is *commiseration*.

Then you start seeing not only everybody else's faults but your faults, 'cause we all have faults. This is *misericordia*: misery of heart. When you get to that stage you stop judging people as much because you realize if *he* has a fault, then I have a fault that's just as bad or worse, so how can I judge my brother? Then St. Bernard quotes Psalm 116 that says "all men are false." Of course, the translation that we don't like is that "all men are liars," that we fool ourselves, that we lie to ourselves. And Bernard says that when we realize this — and he quotes Psalm 116 again, "Blessed in the eyes of the Lord is the death of His Chosen One" — we die a death to ourselves that leads to knowledge of the other person. *Then* we begin to love the other person and that leads to the third degree of knowledge which is love of God. It's very clear Johannine spirituality, which says, "How can we love the God we do not see if we cannot love the brother that we *do* see?"

Spirituality is extremely practical, and this is really what happens in everybody's life. Maybe it happens here quicker, but then we have the luxury of having a schedule that is geared around prayer and not work. How many people in the world have that luxury? Not very many. How lucky we are to be monks! I'm sure that if a man knew all the things that were going to happen to him as a married man, some of the sufferings and agonizing he's gonna go through, he might have thought twice about getting married. Same thing with a monk. I'm sure if God would have let us see some of the things we'd have to go through we'd run the other way. So we all have this. Maybe the monk has it earlier and has it more intensely, but sooner or later everybody's gonna have that experience.

Why wait? God became a man, a person with skin and arms and legs like us. I think it's Gregory that called it "the garment of skin." Well, what a shame to wait at death's door for this relationship to begin. Heaven can begin now. Even St. Paul says that we now have the "first fruits," and we are growing in the spirit. So this garment of skin that's just a covering has already been redeemed by God; all we have to do is go along with that redemption and say "yes." Why wait? Why not have a relationship with God now, because the closer we are to God, the closer we are to one another, and the more we can love one another.

Brother Francis

As an Augustinian I wouldn't have grown as quickly as I have here. How I would have grown, I mean, who knows? Who knows what would have happened out there? I couldn't think of myself as anything other than a monk. When I go into town I feel like a fish out of water. Oh sure! This is home.

† † †

Father Anthony

Entered New Clairvaux - June 19, 1972

Although I was aware of Father Anthony through seeing him in church and scooting about the monastery grounds on his custom-built bicycle, I never really got to know him until I did an interview and photo session about his pottery. What I discovered was an intense, serious-minded individual coupled with the naïveté and childlike wonderment of a true artist, who expresses his God-given gifts through pottery.

Anthony's path leading to the front gate of New Clairvaux has been an amazing one, taking him through some rather rough waters in life. From his early years in Philadelphia through the changes that led him to become a Trappist, we learn firsthand how God intervenes in the lives of those who are called to religious life. And like many of his fellow brothers who have navigated those same choppy seas, he emerged a stronger and more enlightened human being for the experience.

Today, Brother Anthony creates his pottery and sells it through the monastery Welcome Center and on the Internet. His interview is a lesson in perseverance, and of listening to one's "Deep Self" along the road of life.

I didn't want to be a priest. I wanted to get married and have a large family. My mom comes from fourteen children in her family, and so it was really wonderful with all the relatives. I thought that was just marvelous! I loved going to grandma and grandpa's house, and interacting with all my cousins and aunts and uncles and so forth, so I wanted to have a big family. Actually, I was thinking in terms of ten or twelve kids, you know, which is part of the reason that I never got married, because I never found a girl who wanted ten or twelve kids [laughing]. But anyway, I didn't wanna be a priest.

My dad's father died when my dad was about twenty years old, and he got the idea that he was gonna go to daily Mass and pray for his dad. So he started when he was twenty years old, and he went until he was ninety [laughing]. He died when he was ninety-one. So my dad getting up and going to daily Mass was a part of my environment. Now, naturally we all went to Sunday Mass with the family, but when I got to be the age for an altar boy, then my dad made sure that I was there on time and didn't fool around and so forth. Naturally I was a serious altar boy.

When I got to confirmation we didn't have a school. I went to a public school, and then I went to CCD after school twice a week, then we got confirmed. That was kind of the "big thing." After confirmation all the rest of my buddies just dropped out of church. I mean, they went on Sundays, but they had nothing else to do with church, and they kind of dropped out of being altar boys. But I stayed on "because of my dad," sort of thing. So I was an altar boy all the way through high school, and I specifically remember it because when I graduated from high school, the pastor purchased my school ring for me, and he said, "I always buy the school ring for anybody that's an altar boy through high school." But nobody else had ever *been* an altar boy through high school [laughing]. I don't think anybody ever was! But he bought my school ring.

I got to be pretty big for an altar boy. Actually, I was only an altar boy on special occasions, then I began to just kind of help out around the church. I mean, I was *always* there! Anything that was going on in church, we went; novenas, rosaries — any kind of event of any sort. Anyway, this went on all the way through college. By that time I think I was an usher. The reason I say this is because church was a very important part of my life.

Then I graduated from college. I did a business and engineering degree, then I left home and went to work in Milwaukee, Wisconsin. That's where I went to Allis-Chalmers, and they sent me all around the country for a two-year training program. I went to visit the various factories that they had, and that's what got me out here to the West Coast. And being a Catholic, no sooner did I arrive in a place when I immediately found out where's the local Catholic church.

Sometime within that two-year period, what I used to do during Lent was I would go to daily Mass, which was a habit that I had from when I was a kid. I remember being in Milwaukee and going for Lent, and then came Easter, and after Easter I said to myself, "Well, why don't I just keep on doing this?" So I was about twenty-four, twenty-five when I decided. From then on I went to Mass every day.

As it turned out, I became a sales engineer in the pump department, specializing in pumps. I was a factory salesman called an "application engineer." By pumps, I mean we made huge industrial pumps. This is not home pumps for your fish pond! If it was mechanical, they made it. They have since gone out of business.

I graduated in June, and about the middle of July I went to a church dance and I met a girl, and we started dating steady for about six weeks. She left to go to Grand Rapids, Michigan, so we would get together when she would come home for a weekend, or I would go over to visit her. It was sort of a weekend kind of deal. Then I left on my training program and went all over the country, so it was a romance by long distance, sort of, or weekends. In fact, when I was in San Francisco she came out for two weeks vacation the summer that I was there. But all of it was a very short time together, and that went on for about a year.

She finished up the nine months of school and got a job in Milwaukee, and went back to living with her folks. I finished up the training around the country and settled in this job as application engineer in Milwaukee, so now the two of us were in Milwaukee and we got engaged at Christmas time. This was the first time we'd been together in the same city, you might say, and it only lasted 'til February [laughing]. It was great, long distance — it was great! But up close on a steady diet it just wasn't gonna work. It was just different, that's all. So we broke the engagement.

Then I began dating regularly. In fact, I was in a Catholic Alumni Club which was a national club for Catholics who have graduated from college. I graduated from college in '57, so this is now the early sixties. The idea was to meet other Catholics in the same educational level and so on, and meet somebody that could be a partner for you.

So there were two or three hundred people in this club in Milwaukee alone. Matter of fact, I was a vice-president for a year, so I knew tons of lovely young ladies! But like I say [laughing], nobody wanted twelve kids. I mean, when you're getting to know one another, you talk about who you are and where you come from and where you wanna go. Now, I didn't know if I *could* have twelve kids, but I was open to duplicating what I experienced as a kid myself. It was wonderful being part of a huge family. I wanted to do the same thing.

So if a girl would respond and say, "Oh no, I only want one or two [laughing]," well I'd say, "That's fine. One or two, that's not gonna work for me." Yeah! And then of course, you know, there's a whole birth control issue. I mean, how're you gonna only have one or two? Well, I'm a good Catholic boy — I'm going to church every morning — I ain't gonna get involved in something that's gonna cause me a problem. There's natural birth control, but you can't be positive.

I also think I needed somebody who was Catholic, but also *seriously* interested in it because an awful lot of people are Catholic, but that means church on Sunday and that's the end of it, you know; marriage, baptisms for kids, and go to church on Sunday. Then religion's put in a closet until the next Sunday, and you go back to church and take it out, and put it back in the closet again. In fact, that was basically the trouble with the girl I was engaged to because I was beginning to become aware of something called Catholic social action — concern for the poor, con-

cern for laborers — and I was just becoming introduced to this, and I was very much interested in finding out more and talking about it. And the girlfriend, she couldn't care less. I mean, she just wasn't interested in any of that kind of stuff. Well, that's not gonna work.

A lot of people were in that position where religion was just . . . . They were happy to be Catholics, and you would consider them good Catholics — they went to church every Sunday — but that was it. There was no social consciousness, no sharing your bread with the hungry and clothing the naked and visiting the sick and so forth. Matter of fact, when we broke up I joined a group called the Young Christian Workers who got together and talked about things and decided on actions and so on. It was an international organization, and they published a booklet you followed from week to week. We would talk about social action and everyone had to agree to do something that week, like maybe go to your local drugstore and ask the druggist why he's selling pornographic magazines, and ask him if he wouldn't mind taking that off the rack. And every week you had to do something like that. Eventually I got to be the leader of a group like that.

So I was Catholic and I was taking it pretty seriously, and the thing that I chose to do rather than going around to the drugstores was to try and bring Christianity to the workplace. I got the idea of bringing Christianity to Allis-Chalmers, and trying to use Christian principles in dealing with people. I got to be a supervisor pretty quick. Soon they found out I had a business background along with an engineering background, and that became more valuable to them than the engineering. I was twenty-five years old at the time, and was the youngest supervisor in Allis-Chalmers at that time. So being a supervisor, I had people to be responsible for, and I immediately began thinking in terms of Christian principles, of being concerned for people as opposed to getting the most out of them, you know, that sort of thing. Instead of using a whip on them, I was concerned to see that they had the proper training and that they understood what they were doing, and if they had problems I would

listen to them and let them know that I was interested in them as people. And that's what I reported back weekly to my Young Christian
Workers meetings.

On my twenty-sixth birthday, a friend of mine from Philadelphia that
I had gone to college with offered me a job with his father's company, so
I went back to Philadelphia and interviewed, and looked the job over.
Then I got to thinking, "What would I *really* like to do?" And I thought
I'd really like to go back to San Francisco. I had the most wonderful
experience in San Francisco. So I quit the job at Allis-Chalmers, and
packed up and went to California.

Now I'm living in San Francisco, and St. Dominic's Parish is a big
Dominican parish, and it's a great big, huge church — takes up a whole
square block. There were about ten or twelve guys living there, 'cause it
was a priory. In fact, Brother John Cullen was in that parish. He was in
the choir.

So I joined the parish. I wanted my box of envelopes [laughing] and
be officially there. In the meantime, I'm still going to daily Mass, and I
began to meet these Dominicans, and they seemed like really nice guys.
I met one particular brother and he asked me if I would help out on
Sunday. He had a little religious goods display that was on wheels and
he'd roll it out. He asked me if I would be there for two Masses and sell
these objects, and I was very happy to do that. I would go to, let's say, the
nine, and then stay for the ten and the twelve. Then he invited me down
into their dining room to have a little lunch, where I got to meet more
of them. And if I would go to Mass and there would be no altar boy, I
would just walk up onto the altar and serve the Masses. So I was active
in the parish, and this went on for not quite two years.

Okay, so now I'm twenty-seven years old and it was Christmas Eve,
and I was waiting to go to Midnight Mass, and I thought, "While I'm
waiting I oughta read a holy book." So I picked up a book by Thomas
Merton. By this time I'd already read his *Seven Storey Mountain*. This was
called *The Waters of Siloe*, and it's all about the Trappist life. So I'm reading through it and all of a sudden out of absolutely nowhere comes this
thought, "I'm twenty-seven and I'm not married. I wonder if this is for
me?" Whereupon I closed the book and went to sleep! But I did wake up
and go to Midnight Mass.

That was Christmas Eve, and then I didn't really give it any active
thought, but it was just kind of hanging around. So it was Lent —
February or March, something like that — and I'm still thinking about
it. Not seriously at all, but it's not going away. So come the beginning of
Lent I said to myself, "I'm gonna really give this some serious thought,
and by Easter I'm gonna either act on it or not."

Now, what I was gonna act on was *religious life*. It wasn't gonna be the Trappists, even though that's what I read about. It was just the idea of religious life. I don't like things lingering too long. Either "yes" or "no" and get on with whatever we're gonna do, but this "being in limbo" thing I don't appreciate very much.

By this time I had come to understand religious life because of the Dominicans, 'cause I had met these people. Now that's important, because you see, I had never *met* religious! I only knew the parish priest, and the parish priest was always by himself. Maybe he had an assistant, but very often they were by themselves — just one man in the parish doing this pastoral stuff — and that never appealed to me. But all of a sudden the idea of community really is what caught me, because the Dominicans weren't one priest running a parish — it was a whole bunch of guys — and that began to look very appealing. And I was thinking to myself, "Boy, wouldn't it be wonderful to be a member of a group of religious who not only would go to Mass every morning like I was doing already, but who were living together and who could talk about their religion?"

That's the one thing that I didn't get to do. Even when I was in the Young Christian Workers, the focus was on social action, and we really didn't talk about God or religion. We just *did it!* And then, of course, once I came to San Francisco there was no such group — it was just Sunday and daily Mass — so I never had anybody to talk to about God and spirituality.

In the meantime, I'm trying to find books in the library on religious life. And sure enough . . . . Well, it was kind of funny how it worked because I was praying about it and thinking about it. On Palm Sunday I did my usual thing: I sold stuff after the two Masses and I went down to the little dining room. And who should be there but the vocational director for the West Coast Dominicans! I'd met him and I knew who he was. We sat down to eat together and he said to me, "Are you happy?" And I said, "Yeah, I'm very happy. But you know, I think I could be happier if I was in religious life [laughing]." And again, I don't know where *that* came from, because it wasn't like I was ready to go see him or anything. I was just interested to find out if I really wanted to do it. But this just came right out of me.

And he said, "Wonderful! Would you be interested in us?" And I said, "Yeah, I think so."

Naturally, he's the vocational director and jumped on it right away. Before I knew it, there were all the application forms and so on. He said to me, "Would you like to be a priest or a brother," and I didn't know what a brother was, so I said a priest. He put me down for entering the priesthood.

104

But what I remember about that was how it "just happened," and going home after that experience and I was just on cloud nine. I was so excited I could hardly stand it! To think that the decision was made, that this was really what I wanted, to try anyway. I didn't know that I wanted it but I certainly wanted to try it. And you know how it is when you finally make a decision; all the back and forth stuff is over and now you're on your way. So it was really exhilarating, and it was one week before the deadline, you know, Palm Sunday being one week before Easter. So that was it. I was going to enter the Dominicans. It was like somebody offering you a million dollars!

Now again, you have to figure I'm a single man in a city. I've no relatives, I've got a few friends by now but I have no ties. Actually, I was living in a boarding house and I didn't even own very much of anything. I had a car, but since I traveled a lot I made a point not to accumulate, so I didn't have a camera, a radio, phonograph equipment, and obviously I wasn't gonna have a television. All I had was clothing and a portable typewriter and my car. I specifically wasn't gonna get anything, because what was I gonna do with it? I mean, how do you move "stuff?" So I traveled very light: everything fit in the Corvair with plenty of room to spare. The only thing that I collected were a few books and art prints, those real inexpensive one dollar/two dollar prints of modern painters like Picasso and Matisse, and I had a whole collection of those. I used to thumbtack them on the walls of my apartment or wherever I was living. So I joined the Dominicans and went through the whole program: one year of novitiate, three years of philosophy and four years of theology. The novitiate was in Thousand Oaks, California. It was where we were first introduced to the life of a Dominican, more like an orientation program. There were twelve of us that started, and six completed the program and made simple vows. Then we went off to St. Albert's College in Oakland, California. St. Albert's College was the House of Studies for the Dominicans, where we did philosophy and theology to prepare for solemn vows and ordination.

I had a mental breakdown about six months after I got to St. Albert's, in the spring, and I had to go to therapy. I mean, I had it bad! I was wiped out. It happened in the Dominican novitiate but I hung on with my bare teeth until I got into the House of Studies, thinking that I would get past all that somehow, you know, things would get better. I got to the House of Studies and started with my studies program, and it didn't get any better, and finally I just couldn't handle it anymore. So I went to sleep, and I didn't wake up for two weeks. I woke up to eat and to go the bathroom and then go back to sleep. Something was obviously wrong, and I ended up going to a psychiatrist for five years.

The young Dominican artist at St. Albert's in Oakland, California.

This had nothing to do with God; this had to do with who I was, and basically I got the message that I *was* what I *did*. I was a *producer*, because coming from an Italian immigrant family we had nothing. I mean, we weren't starving but we were poor, and you wanted to get ahead. That's my dad saying, "Someday if you practice the piana you'll make a lot of money." Well, that was one way of getting ahead, or studying hard and getting a good job. So it was like "you were gonna get there, you were gonna be somebody if you *produced* and if you made a lot of money."

Well, you can separate the two; money from production. Maybe you didn't make a lot of money but you still had to produce. So I was a producer.

The way I could be accepted in life was to produce, and I produced! I was an efficiency expert; if I wasn't producing I was telling other people how to produce. I mean, that was my thinking, see, how to do things faster, better, easier and make more money at 'em.

So I get into the Dominican novitiate and they hand me a broom and tell me to sweep the pavement, and I'm thinking to myself, "A little broom to sweep the pavement? Why don't I put two brooms together? I can get this job done!" So I'm there putting two three-foot push brooms together. You can push six feet as fast as three feet, and get the job done in half the time!

I'm putting these two brooms together and the novice master comes along and says, "What are you doing?"

I said, "I'm putting these two brooms together so I can get this job done better."

"No, no, no, no! Don't do that! Just sweep with one broom."

Well, I couldn't believe it! I *could not* believe it! So what he was doing was, he was not allowing me to produce, and for the rest of the novitiate there was nothing to produce. I mean, the most we could produce was sweeping the pavement; there was nothing else. And so here I was in a situation where I had no way *to* produce. Well, that meant I didn't exist — I had no identity — and that's pretty hard on ya, and I didn't see the end of it. I didn't know what to do. Then I just began to fall apart. I gave up; I just went to sleep. In a sense I died. Then I went to a psychiatrist and I began to tell him what was going on with me, and gradually we began to look at things and I began to find out, "Oh, *that's* what this is all about. *That's* who I am!"

Well, I am not *what* I do. What I do comes out of me, but that's not *who* I am. And if suddenly I was incapacitated and had to lay in bed for the rest of my life, that doesn't make me any less a person, but I'm sure not gonna be producing very much! So you have to face yourself. That's what I needed to face, to see where I got the messages from and why I thought of myself in those terms, and how I had to give that up and pick up with a new message.

I would say it's an ongoing process because I was born with this; this is what I inherited from my folks. In my mother's womb I was expected to someday be a producer. It's messages. You know, they talk about the tapes? This is the tape that was recorded when you were a kid and you keep playing it all through your life. So you have to erase the tape and put a new tape in. Or now, with computer programing, you put a program in the computer and then that's what you get. Well, you have to take that program out and put a new program in. So with yourself it's the same kind of thing.

I'm sixty-four years old now but it's still part of who I am, except that now I know it, so I make sure that I keep it in balance. Being a producer is a *good* thing, it's just that it has to be kept in check, and my knowing that's not the full range of who I am. But yeah, that's very, very important, and not just something that *I* experienced. I would say a lot of people experience that same kind of thing. And because I'm aware of it I've been able to help a lot of people deal with that to some extent, at least let 'em know that's a large part of peoples' problems in trying to be comfortable and happy being who they are.

That can happen in religious life, it can happen outside of religious life; some set of circumstances can just crush you and you can no longer handle them with your tape and you're wiped out. But if somehow you can get help, then you can begin to build up a new understanding of yourself. So that's one way, the crisis that wipes you out. And then we often talk about people have to reach their rock bottom. It's almost like an alcoholic: when an alcoholic ends up in a ditch he might decide, "Hey, maybe this is not a good thing to be doing. I'll go to AA or something or other."

The other way, I would say — maybe a little easier way — is if people are interested in prayer, because if you are willing to go to prayer on some sort of regular basis, things will begin to come up and you can begin to look at them in prayer and gradually make changes and grow. But nobody ever told me about that. Prayer for me was prayer books, prayer cards. I used to carry around a wad of prayer cards in my wallet, and while I was riding the bus some place I'd take out my wallet and take out the prayer cards and I'd start reading all these prayers to St. Anthony, St. Anne, St. Jude, the Holy Spirit novenas, St. Joseph, the Blessed Mother — I had an endless number of these prayer cards. But in those days in the back of the church there would be tons of them, you know. So that was prayer. Then you go to church and you say the rosary or you follow your missal. But there was no introduction to any kind of quiet prayer, talking to God prayer or just being quiet, like now we have Centering Prayer and meditative kind of prayer, what we call *lectio divina* where we read the Scriptures and let that speak to you. Well, nobody ever said anything about that to me.

What I learned a little bit in the Dominicans was meditative prayer where you think of some mystery: Jesus on the Cross, and you picture it and then you smell it and so forth, hear the sounds of the people and even the flies flying around and all that kind of stuff. Well, that's a form of meditation, but I don't know if that's gonna lead you to finding out who you are and what's going on with you. I'm thinking more in terms of prayer where you go to God and you sit down and you say, "God, something is bothering me. Do you mind if we talk this over?" And then you grow on the inside. But you've gotta do that on a regular basis, and there's gotta be a certain amount of time. You don't do that in five minutes, you know, you gotta set aside time; probably have a place. It's gotta be routine, which means your whole life has gotta be sort of organized such that it's more of a routine. Well, how many people in our society can do that or *will* do that? They'll go to the gym and work out on a regular basis, but they're not too likely to go to prayer on a regular basis.

So I would think that mostly, if people are going to "get it" [finding your true self] they are gonna get it because of a crisis, some kind of wipe out: death in the family, serious job loss, an injury, some narrow escape from disaster of one kind or another. Then they realize that they've got to change, that there's gotta be some kind of serious changes if they're gonna survive.

A lot of people that I know now are pursuing it. They somehow have learned that there is a mystical aspect and they want it. They go to workshops, retreats or come to Vina, or they read and they look for it. So they'll get it. If you want it, you go get it. But it's not gonna be handed to anybody on a platter. I think there is a hunger, but I don't think most people know what to do with that hunger or how to fill it.

I always had this great desire to look at pictures. I had tried to draw in school, and my drawing was nothing; I couldn't draw anything worth a damn! I'd make an airplane — this was during the second world war — and you could barely tell it was an airplane. You saw the propeller but . . . .

Somewhere I got the idea that in order to be an artist you had to be born with it. I never heard anybody learning it; nobody said anything about teaching it. Either you had it or you didn't, and I definitely didn't have it, so I just never tried anything beyond grade school drawing. But it didn't discourage my art appreciation at all. I got into college and it was the same thing. I was forever looking at art books and going to museums, and I had my collection of paper paintings that I kept rolled up and took with me wherever I went.

When I got to Oakland it turned out they had an art studio that some previous students made up in the attic of St. Albert's College. One great big, huge room with skylights was a painting studio, and there were easels and paint and brushes — everything you need. And lots of paintings that the guys had done and left behind. Nobody was actively working; it was a class and then they graduated. And then I came.

It suddenly occurred to me, "I wonder if I could do something?" By this time I'd come to appreciate the fact that there was such a thing as abstract art, which didn't have to look like anything, so you didn't have to learn how to draw; all you had to do was play with color, and I loved color. I could go to an art museum or gallery, look at a painting and tell you what it needed, you know, a little orange down here and a little blue up there. So I had developed a sense of what I liked, and I figured, "Well shucks, I can put color on a canvas. That shouldn't be terribly hard."

So one day I just shut the door — I didn't want anybody to see this private experience — and tried it. I took a canvas, took some paint, squeezed it out and I painted my first painting. It was just an abstract painting of color on canvas. I was so excited that I don't think anybody who takes heroin could have had a "high" more than I had with seeing the results of my first painting. I was so turned on that I became an addict [to painting]. I was so excited that I could do it! So having had that experience I just continued. I started knocking out paintings two and three a day [laughing]. I had a lot of catching up to do. It was like an assembly line.

We had a little carpenter shop and I started making frames, and hanging them up. Of course, the first place I hung 'em was in this art room, but then they began to filter down into the rest of the house. People would come to visit and they would see them and like them, and I would give 'em to them or sometimes they'd give me a donation. Well, once I started having donations then I could buy materials, and I was on my way!

My idea of art is that you create beauty at some level. It may look ugly at first glance but if you look at it long enough you'd see there's beauty in it somewhere. Thanks be to God I'm very comfortable with who I am, and people can shoot holes in me and it doesn't make any difference. Where I really got a big dose of that was in my artwork. Somebody would come along and say, "Wow! That's terrific! That's the best thing I've ever seen," and I'd be so high you couldn't find me.

Then the next guy would come along, see the same thing and he'd say, "What's that? My little nephew could do better than that!" Well, you'd have to pick me up, you couldn't find me on the ground. I'd be a puddle of nothing I'd be so wiped out. And it was driving me crazy. I mean, I couldn't keep up with it. What even puzzled me more was how can the same painting end up with such different extremes? Is that a good painting or not a good painting?

Then I began to study all that, and what I ended up learning was that people were actually telling about *themselves*: what they liked and didn't like was revealing themselves. It really had nothing to do with me. Once I was able to separate all that stuff, then I could say, "Here comes Charlie. He's gonna like this painting." And sure enough, he likes that painting. Why? Because Charlie likes *blue* paintings. All I had to do was put blue on a canvas and Charlie's gonna like it. I knew that, and I had everybody figured out [laughing]. People were so predictable it was unbelievable! But they were revealing themselves. It had nothing to do with me. But that's how I got my kicks. I was somebody running around looking for approval so that I could have a place in the world, which is a pretty sad state of affairs, but I had to deal with that.

Along came the opportunity to go to school during the summer time. We were close to the University of California [Berkeley] so I went there and took some art classes, and *then* I learned how to draw. I also took a course at Holy Names College in Oakland, and while I was there I decided to take a pottery course. Once I tried clay, I just really fell in love with clay. I loved painting, but when I touched clay that was just so exciting! And we had a wheel and a kiln at St. Albert's, so I resurrected all this stuff and I started doing pottery. Then it began to be a problem, because what was it going to be: painting or clay? I actually moved the painting studio to a basement area and then I would have to decide, "Now should I go to the attic or the basement?" And for awhile I was going to both, but it got to the point where the clay was drawing me more and more, so eventually I just stopped painting; clay took over and I started doing pottery.

Along about the time after Vatican II, when the changes in the church began to take place, one of the important changes was you could use pottery chalices in the liturgy. Up to this time you could only use gold and silver, so immediately it opened a door to pottery chalices. It so happened that the newspaper photographer for the Oakland Catholic paper, the *Voice*, knew that I was making pottery. So when it came time that the changes were going to be announced in the newspaper, he thought he would add a human interest story such as me making chalices: "Dominican Priest Makes Pottery Chalices."

So he ran the story, and then the story got picked up by the San Francisco newspaper, and I remember my picture was on the front page that day looking at one of my pottery chalices. It must have been around 1970. National Catholic News Service picked it up from there. All of a sudden I started getting letters saying, "Where do we buy your pottery chalices?" And you see, this is the ground floor now! So I decided to go into business. I did a landslide business in pottery chalices all over the nation [ten a week @ $40.00 each]. Everything belonged to the Order, but as far as my art supplies I didn't scrimp on anything [laughing].

After two years of theology I was ordained a priest, but I had two more years of theology to complete. I was called a student priest; I could say Mass and preach but I couldn't hear confessions until I finished my studies. After completing theology, I was sent to St. Dominic's parish in Benicia, California, and did a nine-month pastoral training program. I spent three days a week working in the parish and the other three days in San Francisco attending classes and reviewing the work I was doing in the parish.

I was two months into that program when I had to give a report to the pastoral training program about what was going on in my situation. And I got up and I remember saying, "I don't wanna be where I am. I don't wanna be a parish priest." So I spent the rest of the nine-month program learning how to be pastorally oriented, but also trying to figure out what I was gonna do.

A friend of mine — a Dominican who I was very close to and I used to talk to him about it — he said, "You know, it sounds like what you like about being a Dominican was the community living," 'cause as a student there were sixty-five people living in the house, and that made a wonderful community life. Well, then I get into the parish and there were three of us: the pastor and an assistant, and I was there as kind of an intern, you might say. But that *wasn't* a community. So when I was telling my friend this, he said, "I think what you really are interested in is the Trappists in Vina, 'cause they're a community and they *live* like a community." I said, "Where's that?"

He had been there a couple of times, so he arranged for us to come on a three-day retreat right after Easter. I think I had written to Brother John Paul before that, the vocations director and guest master, saying that I was interested in the life. Well, to my surprise, while I was here on the retreat, John Paul had gone ahead and arranged for interviews. So I remember talking to Father Thomas, Father Joseph James and Father Paul Jerome. I talked to all of them and I told them out and out, "I don't really want to be a monk. I don't even know what a monk is, and I've never thought about being a monk, but I *don't* wanna be a parish priest! So it's like I'm backing into here. I really wanna be here, in a sense of I wanna do what you guys do — I don't even know what that is — but it doesn't matter to me as long as you're religious living in a community and you're here all the time, that's what I'm looking for."

So they said, "Okay, fine. That's all right. God brings people here in many different ways. Come and try it out." That was all I needed. I got permission from my provincial, and the following June when we graduated from the pastoral training program I was free to come.

I was gonna be here a month to do an observership — that's the first thing you do — and if that works you're supposed to leave, think it over and settle your business and come. And I said, "Well, I don't have any business to settle. If it works I'll just stay on." So it worked. It *really* worked! Actually, it worked from the first day that I came here on retreat, and I wanna tell you what worked about it was Vincent — that's my Dominican friend — Vincent and I were walking down the south road here, and we passed the first field, and it had been just newly plowed. And I looked at that field and I said, "My goodness. Isn't that beautiful? Look at that plowed field!" You know, you could see all the row marks made by the plow in perfect parallel lines, and earth turned over and ah, geez, it looked to me like a huge canvas that somebody had painted this wonderful picture on, you know. And I was just . . . . I was like a kid in a toy shop or something [laughing], seeing all these tractors and pruning towers and so on.

Now, I guess this would have been my engineering background coming out and my artistic background, plus the fact it was a community. Everybody was very friendly. It was a youthful community. I was thirty-eight; most of the guys were forty, forty-two, so I fit right into the group. I felt really welcomed, and it was terrific. I just thought it was the most wonderful thing imaginable! So that's how I got to Vina.

Although I happened to be a priest, I nevertheless had to start all over; there was a two-year novitiate. Now, a curious thing actually happened. Well, first of all, there was about nine months of being a postulant then I became a novice, so it was not quite three years when Father Thomas said to me one day, "I guess we have to think about your taking solemn vows." And I said, "Oh? Are we gonna *think* about it?"

I didn't think there was anything to think about. I thought it was an open-and-shut case. I mean, it was just obvious that "I'm here," you know? But when he said that, it caught me up short. Actually, I joked about it a little bit. I said, "Okay, I'll think about it," which I wasn't planning on doing until he said that. But when he said that, I *started* thinking about it. And in those days there was kind of a movement — sort of like a fad almost — but the movement at that particular time was, "You have to listen to your 'deep self.' Go inside of you." We haven't said much about that lately, but anyway I said, "Oh, I guess I should listen to my 'deep self' and see what my 'deep self' says about this."

I distinctly remember going and sitting in a room by myself and saying, "Okay, this is it 'deep self.' Now I wanna hear what I'm supposed to

The monastic "flower child."

do." And my "deep self" said, "Go back to the Dominicans," and that came as a real surprise to me. So I asked my "deep self," "Would you mind repeating that [laughing]?" I didn't know why I wanted to go back to the Dominicans but my "deep self" said, "Go back to the Dominicans."

So I went to Father Thomas and said, "Guess what? My "deep self" said I should go back to the Dominicans." He was completely taken off guard, as was Father Paul Jerome the novice master. So before I actually finished the novitiate I contacted the provincial of the Dominicans and said I'd like to come back. They said, "Great! Wonderful! Love to have you back."

I got assigned to Seattle. I thought that was the end of Vina. I was there about two months and I said, "No, I have to go back to Vina."

So I wrote a letter to Father Thomas and he said, "I talked to the council. You can come back, but stay out a full year, and if a year from now you still wanna come back, just come on back." So that's what I did. I stayed out for a full year.

The "deep self" told me to leave because the importance of leaving was that I got to go back to the Dominican House where I had spent all those wonderful years, and say good-bye to it and close it up. I had never closed up. In psychological terms they talk about closure with people, situations, things, places — you need to give closure to things before you

114

can really go on to the next thing — and I had never done that. I mean, I left St. Albert's to go to Benicia, I left Benicia to come to Vina — I never said good-bye to anybody — I just left. That's all. There were no good-bye parties, no farewells.

So that's what happened. I had to do that but I didn't know I had to do it. So when I came back to Vina I said, "Hey 'deep self,' what was that all about?" But it was "deep self" moving me another step along the way. My history always seems to be going to the next thing that I needed to do, and that became clear and I did it insofar as I turned my life over to God and wanted to do whatever God wants for me. But you know, God doesn't write you a letter. A lot of people come to me and say, "I don't know what I'm supposed to do or what I should do? I don't know what my vocation is." And I say, "Well, a simple answer to that is, 'What do *you* wanna to do?'" If you know what you wanna do, that's what God wants you to be doing because God is putting all the impulses and talents in you, and you just be you. I have the intellect, body and creative hands so I use all of those, and they move me in a certain way, and I follow that movement. I'm not gonna do something that I'm not good at, so I end up being artistically-oriented and doing artwork. Well, where does that come from? I figure it comes from God because I trace it back to when I was the littlest kid. When God created us He created us with certain characteristics.

I came to Vina as an accomplished potter/painter. When I came here there was nothing like that going on at all. In the monastic lifestyle there is no such thing as a hobby. In those days it was even more strict, so you'd never use the word *hobby*. It was just that somehow I obviously had an artistic bent, and art is a good thing so it's all right to be an artistically oriented person. But to figure out how you're gonna do it is something else, you know. So it was kind of walking a very careful line between what's okay and what's not. A hobby is definitely *not* okay; art *is* okay. Now how are we gonna work this? Money is there if you can figure out how to integrate the whole thing and make everybody comfortable with it.

I got permission to do a little bit of painting. Then I gave a homily and mentioned that I had done pottery. Well, there was a visitor here and her husband was the art teacher at a local high school and he taught pottery. It so happened that he was getting a new kiln and he had all this old clay that he had to get rid of, and he asked if I wanted this old clay. I asked the abbot and he said, "Fine," so I got delivered this big pile of clay, and that started me on clay here at Vina.

We happened to have an old broken-down wheel that I found which

Doing a bit of gardening.

was used kind of like a little lathe. So then I needed a kiln. At first I was firing in a metal barrel that we had for an incinerator. You could put pottery in it with sawdust and light the sawdust. As the sawdust burned, it fires the pottery, very similar to what the Indians did. The pots were fragile and they weren't matured by any stretch of the imagination, and you couldn't glaze them that way, but that was the first thing I did.

The only problem was how much was I an artist and how much was I a monk? In other words, did I come here to be an artist and find this to be a convenient setting for me to be an artist? Or did I come here to be a monk who happened to do artwork? Well, *I* didn't even know the answer to that, but they were very much concerned about that. So one

116

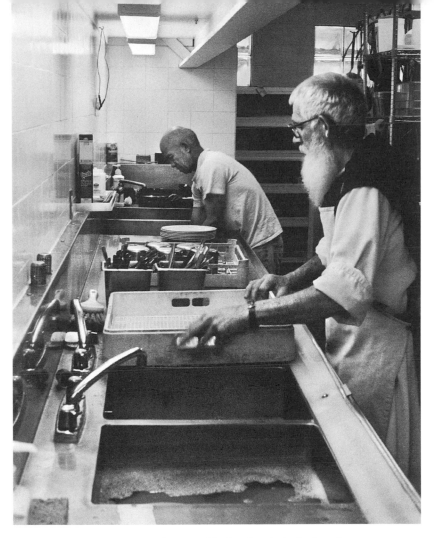

Anthony giving Father Harold a hand with the kitchen chores.

of the things I had to do was to do no artwork for a year; absolutely nothing. And it was kind of like, "Let's see if you can do it," and I was curious to see if I *could* do it, too. I was a professional artist, although I never thought of myself in those terms.

I survived a year. It was no problem, which indicated that I really was a monk first, and if art was available I would certainly engage in it. If it was not available that's all right; I could live without art. So I passed the test!

The same high school art teacher who gave me the clay also gave me a small electric kiln that I was able to fix up and fire the pots. Now the next step was to be able to glaze the pots, but for this I needed to purchase raw materials to mix up glazes, and this meant I needed money which I did not have.

I hit on a plan to pick up black walnuts that we have all over the property which only the squirrels cared about. I heard that they sold for $2.00 for a potato bag full, so I got permission to pick them up and sell them, and use the money for glaze materials.

I must have picked up millions of black walnuts! It was a lot of work for two dollars to pick up a bagful of black walnuts. But remember, we're talking about 1973 when that was a lot of money. By proposing that I pick up walnuts and use that money for glazes, it sort of made it easy for everybody. In other words, I wasn't being given money for a hobby; I was working it out. I collected something like $400, which was a terrific amount of money. I really went at it with a vengeance! I was super excited about what I was doing and I poured every bit of energy into it.

When I had the money available to use for pottery supplies, the first thing I did was build a kiln. In fact, I even bought a new electric wheel. I bought a kit that was available at the time so I had a nice new kiln and a wheel, and I was in business! This was '76/'77. The first year I worked in a barn where there was no heat, so come winter time I was freezing. Then I found the old milking parlor which was used for storage, and I asked for permission to clean that out and use it. Then I moved in there.

I would just make pottery and fire it up and play around with glazes. I had a shelf where I put the pottery with a big sign saying, "If You See Anything You Like, It's Yours," and it just went. Everybody had pieces in their rooms and was giving it to their friends and relatives and anybody that came to visit, and I made cups for the community. And here again, donations would come in for pottery. I kind of had this fund that I could use for pottery.

Brother Paul, the business manager, suggested that maybe I would like to try this as a business, so we set it up as a business. Then I started to sell it. It's down in the Welcome Center and also mail order. It's like everything else: one person hears about it and tells somebody else, and the first thing you know you make a contact. As far as the monastery is concerned, now I am on the official work list. It goes down as pottery. Of course, I'm also the electrician and I prepare suppers and do house cleaning and help in the harvest, so I do a lot of things. I have to do all the important things before I do the pottery, obviously.

I don't make casseroles or functional plates or stuff like that. It's generally little shapes which could be mostly vases. The first thing I'm doing I'm playing. I'm not working [laughing]. I have this basic theory that says there's two kinds of activity that we're all engaged in all the time, and that is play and work. Now, work is anything you do that you do out of

Monastery transportation à la Anthony.

necessity basically to live. Then after you've covered that, then your activities are play. So insofar as it's play, I don't really *make* pottery; pottery happens in the course of my play. No two are ever alike, and I have no interest in two alike. That would be *making* them, see?

One of the real delights is opening the kiln and seeing what you get. It's just like Christmas! You don't know what you're gonna get and it's very, very exciting. It's a kick!

All the way back to the beginning of my art career I tied art to psychology because I learned that what we produce comes out of our inner being. If you look at your productions you can learn something about yourself. I worked out a theory of a symbolic language so I could come back and look at my artwork and say, "Ah ha! That's where I'm at. That's what's going on with me."

Now one of the most basic things that I learned about pottery was

Dipping a pot in glaze.

Pots awaiting firing in the kiln.

"It's just like Christmas!" Anthony removes a newly-fired pot from the kiln with a child-like wonder.

that pottery is either male or female shaped. A tall, thin pot is male because it's phallic. A nice round, squatty pot is female because that's round and that's like a womb. Now, if I sit down today and make two dozen pots, and I didn't know what I was making, then I look at them and I say, "I'm in a female place and therefore I made female pots," or "I'm in a male place and I made male pots." That tells me where I'm at today on the spectrum of my own psychology. I also know that it's better for me to be in a female place because when I get too male I start getting pushy [laughing]. I start telling people what to do and where to go and how to do it. Generally, people don't like that. That's my male function, the critical.

My female side is when I'm open and accepting and noncritical. That's a much better place for me to be as a person interacting with other people. People prefer when I'm in that more easy-going place. I've learned that, so the pottery and artwork has helped me to understand where I'm at and then make the necessary adjustments so that I can live my life in a way that's more enjoyable. Every person is made up of the male and female qualities, not only artists. We've all got it going. I think it's a good thing if we understand ourselves. We can fit better into life and the people we're surrounded with.

I'm aware that the pottery has a lot of appeal to people because it comes from a monk in a monastery. It's marked as New Clairvaux pottery made by Father Anthony, and it's signed on the bottom, "New Clairvaux." My personal symbol is a cross with a flower. The flower is Anthony because Anthony in Greek means flower, so it's a combination of a flower and a cross, which is me and God working together.

Basically, creation is intended to be beautiful. I have an instinct and desire to want to create, and maybe that's just my own natural need. I don't create children so I create pottery, and here's all these "little kids" running around the place, you know, going off into the world. And there's a certain sense of delight. My pottery brings delight to people: I like the thought of that.

† † †

Father Anthony can be reached at the monastery web site www.maxinet.com/trappist. This gets you to the New Clairvaux web page, then click on Father Anthony's name and an article on his pottery will appear. Click again for the cyber gallery.

Father Dominic

Studied at New Clairvaux - 1989 to 1993

When I was interviewing monks at New Clairvaux in 1991, there were two Trappists visiting from Africa who were studying at the American monastery. Brother Dominic was one of them, and consented to talk with me. I have rarely come across a more positive, upbeat soul in any walk of life! His viewpoint on the world stems from a love burning deep within that has been forged by the Holy Spirit. In a heavy accent punctuated often by an exuberant laugh and broad smile, I was amazed how this man in his early thirties had gained such a remarkable wisdom at such an early stage of life.

But as is oftentimes the case, this wisdom had come at a price. Brother Dominic is a poignant example of a Christian who, like many of us at one time or another, suddenly finds himself in a crisis of faith. That he was able to withstand his test of faith is attributed solely to the work of the Holy Spirit, who responded because Dominic sought the truth and received it.

Dominic has since been ordained a priest, and resides at Our Lady of Victory Abbey, Kenya, East Africa.

Somehow I felt from childhood that I wanted either to be a priest or something like that. I used to read spiritual books in my father's home about the saints when I was young, so somehow the idea came from my childhood.

I could have been anything else I wanted to be. For example, normally one would go to what they call the minor seminary, but I attended just public secondary school. And still, I felt all the way through that something of a religious life was in me. I didn't have problems of decision. Right from childhood, as I was growing up, I did not have to sit down and say, "Do I want to be this or that?" At school I was studying all the subjects; mathematics, chemistry and everything, but still my ideas were basically religious. My mind is kind of inclined to philosophical thinking, you see. The whole setting of my mind somehow deals with ideal things and ultimate goals.

So I attended a Catholic primary school, and every Tuesday we had a priest come in to say Mass for us. When I joined the secondary school — what you call high school here — I used to attend Mass before I went to school every day, and the parish priest one time asked me, "Would you like to become a priest?" I said, "Oh, of course I would [laughing]!" I went with the priest to see the vocations director of the diocese, then I kept contacts throughout secondary school. From high school I joined the major seminary in 1979.

In the third year of philosophy I was going to the library and I came across a little booklet, *White Monks,* so I read about the white monks. I was a sacristan at the time and I had two assistants. We used to share our lives and our thoughts. One wanted to become a Jesuit. I don't remember so much what the other wanted to become. Then I told them I wanted to become a monk. They told me to go and get more formation from the Benedictine Sisters of the Blessed Sacrament in eastern Uganda during the vacation, so I went there in 1980. I didn't know the difference between the Benedictines and the Trappists then.

I went to see the sisters. They told me, "There's a new monastery being constructed in Nairobi, Kenya, by the Benedictines. Possibly you could go there and see the life." So I went to Kenya to visit the Benedictines. Oh, they were so happy to see me! They said, "Okay, we shall consider your case. Go back and finish your exams." I was doing my final paper in philosophy at the time.

Between philosophy and theology there was a pastoral year, so I was admitted to the Benedictines, but after a few months I saw that what I had read of the *white monks* was different from what I was experiencing in the Benedictine life. Somehow I saw my ideals could be realized best in a Trappist monastery. I took up the matter with my spiritual director and he said, "No, God calls you here, so you should stay as a Benedictine." So I stayed for a year and finished the postulancy, but my life was uneven with the Benedictine style. I could sense that most of my life was somehow contradictory with what was there. I talked with the superiors and told them, "Let me try the Trappist life." I left the Benedictines on the seventh of November, 1983, and joined the Trappists, but I had to go back to zero; I had to start again with postulancy and the novitiate.

When I joined the Trappists I saw that it was somehow fitting in with my life, but the novitiate was very tough. I never saw anything tougher than the Trappist novitiate [laughing]! We wake up at quarter-past three, as here. Then twenty-five past three we start the Vigils. We have Mass at quarter to five. Immediately after Mass, the novices have to go to the garden to water the vegetables and this and that, and it could be very cold, you know, cold wind blowing all the time, but we endured it. So I mean it was very tough in that way. But one of the things which I learned was that in the seminary I had read about grace, okay? And in the Benedictines I had read about grace and God's Providence in books, but I never felt how grace works in my blood. Now here in the Trappist novitiate I came to know that every day, to take any step, I needed grace, you see, to keep existing there and to get through the novitiate. That's when I knew without grace it was not possible trying to become a Trappist; it just was not possible! That's the realization. So after the novitiate I said, "Yes, there is a Providence and there is grace!"

Then my superiors, after my final vows in 1989, they wanted me to become a priest. Now, it is the custom of the Trappists to send their monks to another monastery if they don't have enough professors. We didn't have enough professors for theology so we had to look for another monastery. I was to go to Mt. St. Bernard in England to have my studies there but they wrote back and said they too, did not have enough professors, and referred us to Vina [New Clairvaux]. So we wrote to Vina and Father Abbot was very happy to receive me.

When you read the *Rule of St. Benedict* and see how the life is lived, there is quite a big difference — there is a big gap — between the *Rule* and the life at the Benedictine monastery where I was. See, *they* are missionaries. St. Benedict *didn't have* the idea of missionary work in writing his *Rule*; it was intended for monks as a kind of contemplative atmosphere in the enclosure. Okay? But, as a Benedictine you have to move around, you teach in universities and in your own parishes. I didn't feel like I was called to that. Yeah, so that was the big thing, you see? All the time I didn't feel I'm called to go to teach in the seminaries or in the universities or to work in any parishes. This wasn't my idea of a monastery.

So when I came to the Trappists I saw that they were closer to the *Rule*, although there still — even when you read the *Rule* of the Trappists — still there is some gap between the *Rule* and the Trappist life. But at least the Trappist life is closer to the *Rule* than the Benedictine missionary life.

I also wanted to find out who Christ was. That was the biggest question in my life. Now, how am I going to find out who Christ is, you know? Christ is a very big problem. Even Christ Himself asked, "Who do men say I am?" Some said, "You are Elijah, or one of the prophets."

When I was in the major seminary, at one time I entered into a crisis of faith whether Christ existed as a human being historically. It was a very serious question for me because if Christ never existed, then I'm believing in nothing! I mean, this is illusion, you see? So how am I going to find Christ historically?

I went to the library and got those big books of those big men — the Church Fathers — to find out the arguments whether Christ existed, and I couldn't come to any conclusion that Christ existed from just mere reading. So how am I to find out whether Christ existed?

I almost gave up the whole thing of Christianity. I wanted to go and join the army at that stage, because if Christ doesn't exist, it is nonsense to believe. But anyway, I opened the Bible one time, just by chance, and I opened to John 14:21. I cannot forget that text. It talks of Jesus manifesting Himself to us: "I will manifest Myself to him who loves My Father and keeps My commandments."

I said, "Wait a minute! If He promised to manifest Himself, then I must wait. Maybe He's going to manifest later on. I don't know." Now the search begins there, the serious search for Christ in my life. So now I want to know exactly who this Christ is, and I must devote my whole life in search for this Christ. But where can I find the place where I can devote my whole energy and being into this search? I have to invest all my strength and my intellectual capacity in this search for Christ. I knew I had to be somewhere in solitude, and that is where the Trappist monastery could provide such an atmosphere. So that's where my search came from. And in the long run, in the monastery, I found out Christ existed, you see?

Nobody can prove to you historically that He did exist. Could be stories, maybe, but there are so many stories which have no foundation. But as He promised — "I will manifest Myself" — that was a great revelation for me. If this never existed in the Bible I would have thrown out all hopes because there is no possible way. But in one's life somehow He manifests. Truth will tell you about Him. But yet, at a certain stage in your life, something has had to happen deep in you so that He can open your eyes, and it will be there, and you will say, "Yes, it is!" You see?

So that happened in my life with the Trappists. I can't say I had a vision, it's not something visible like I saw Mary or St. Joseph. No, this is kind of what you call "insights." It's just something you feel. So from there on I started to understand, "Yes, there is a Christ," and arguing from that fact then the Bible begins to make more sense to you, you see? Then you start to understand that, "Oh, since I have understood *who* He is, then what He said is true!" It's like connecting things, here and there. Now things fall into place, they are making sense, you see?

It is said in the Bible we are made in the image of God. As you grow in the spiritual life, by meeting people this awareness gets deeper. When you meet a person something has to touch you. This spirit develops in you that each person is very unique, any given person, despite their weaknesses. Every single person has weaknesses — the dark side of a person — but despite all that the beauty of a human person is inexhaustible, and then you come to know clearer that a person is made in the image of God.

For example, Hitler. Okay, you have to ask yourself why a person behaves like this. You may say that he's totally responsible for everything, but you have to go into his background. There could be so many reasons which causes this man to turn into that ugly thing. Maybe I would have done the same, but despite all the ugliness, if you ask, "Does Hitler want to be happy?" — nobody wants to be unhappy, you see? If he doesn't want to be unhappy, then somehow he is seeking happiness, and happiness is God Himself. He may be confused and do all kinds of crazy things, but you may find that maybe there's something wrong in him which we do not know now. But he's a human being, and maybe if he was given a chance — if he was not killed but maybe was captured and given a chance — possibly he would have repented. God is very merciful.

Look at St. Paul. Paul was persecuting the Church and was executing and imprisoning the people. He was there when they were stoning Stephen, and he was thinking, "I'm working for God," and was convinced he was doing so! You *could* judge him: "Oh, this is a murderer. He is killing the people." But there is something in his perception of reality that is different from me and you. So that's why we cannot judge exactly, "Oh, that one is in hell or that one." No, we cannot do that. There is some good in him. We may not be able to see it, but there is. True. Yeah, sure.

When you study Eastern religions, at the depth of it there is something very deep in those religions. For example, take a look at all these religions we know, Hinduism or Islam or Christianity, just by seeking happiness and peace these religions all say that you can be peaceful *somehow*. Or take any human being who knows nothing about religion; somehow in himself he seeks happiness. But if we're asking, "What is peace?" eventually you're headed for God.

In the monastery we are human beings just like any other human being. That's one problem people have in the world is to idealize monastic life. Monastic life is not angelic. That's the illusion, okay? Only angels can live angelic lives [laughing] because they *are* angels by nature. Human beings have brief human life. That's the only way it works. So in the monastery there is life just like any other family. Take *your* family;

129

quarrels and misunderstandings are inevitable, and you are going to have these clashes here, and this and that. This happens, too, in the monastic situation. For example, you are supposed to love your brother, okay? You may find that he is a very difficult brother to love. Yeah. This is human. I mean, the brother might be looking at you with contempt always, but you have to love this brother, and you say, "I *must* love this brother." But sometimes it is true that you have neglected the brother's needs, you see? So all this happens. Yes. And then you have to work on that: "Now, how I can I love this difficult brother?" By yourself without grace, you cannot, and that's when you can say, "Let us talk over the matter with my brother or my difficult friend." You tell him: "I find this very difficult. I find a problem here with you. Let's talk the matter over and then we see which direction to take." Yeah, all these things happen in here just as in the world.

So we're not in the monastery because we're a saint or something like that. It's just we are trying to achieve our vocation as a Christian that way, and you're going to clash with your brothers always. But this clashing has to teach you something. It's a question of, "How do you handle and interpret the confusion, insecurity, clashes and difficulties?" There is always a message, you know, in everything that happens to you, even if you may think that the event is bad. So in all these quarrels and difficulties, when I sit down and think, there is a message there.

When I look at my life there are many miserable things which I thought maybe were bad. When I left the Benedictines, I didn't contact the Trappists first that I was coming. Between the Benedictines and the Trappists I was hanging between heaven and earth, okay? "Where am I going to go next" and "Maybe I can do this or that." It kind of looked miserable leaving the place where I had been for some time, just like maybe for the first time you are leaving your parents and you are going to support yourself economically. This is the first time you're going to be involved in your own life and it may be very difficult to see how you are going to exist without the economic support of your parents. But in the course of time, you can say it is *good* I broke off from my parents, otherwise if I was always clinging to them I would never have grown; I would never have developed into who I am.

So, when you look at your history and try to put things in order and look at the miserable things you thought were miserable at that time, you may find that they are throwing light to the way you are now. And you can say that, "At this point, if this miserable thing did not happen to me, maybe I would have been here or there or would never have gone in that direction." So you look at all these things, and connecting them you say, "Oh, so what happened there had meaning in reference to something

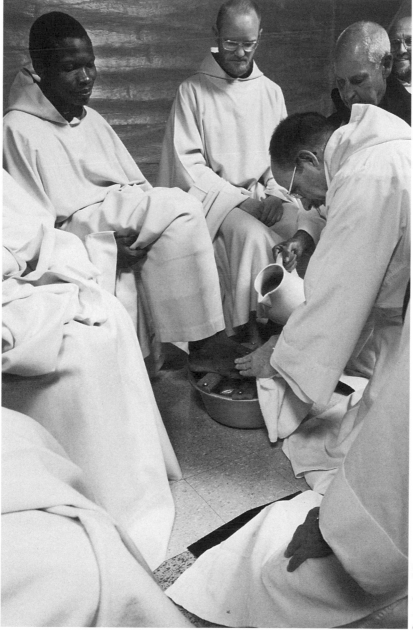

Abbot Thomas Davis washes the feet of then Brother Dominic during Holy Thursday ceremonies, re-enacting Jesus washing the feet of the Apostles at the Last Supper.

which was to come for me."

In that way you have to reflect on your experiences. All of them! Don't hide any experience from your consciousness, even if it is a bad experience. You have to bring it in front of you and accept it as part of you: "I stole so many things" or maybe "I took some bribe." Everything has some significance.

Contemplation is the biggest thing in the Trappist life. People have different definitions of contemplation, but I understand it as opening my heart to God to receive love, enjoy it and let it flow through me to other human beings to bring peace and joy in their lives. It's not a question of closing myself up or introversion; I must be aware of my brothers anywhere in the world. Human beings are one, in a sense. That's one big thing in Eastern religions, you have this Brahman where the whole of reality somehow is one thing; the "world soul" embraces everything. Although there is truth there, my interpretation also is that *you* are part of *me*. You may not be aware that you are part of me, but it is so.

For example, if I wish you bad luck and miseries, I'm destroying myself and I'm destroying you. You are part of me, so you're part of me in a very real sense *and* from a Christological point of view; the Body of Christ. We are parts of the one Body. You could be the eye and I could be the foot! So you can't say that I'm a monk for the monastery alone and I'm hanging around here with my own things in my head. No, it's not a question of being "in the head," you see, that's a wrong idea also; that's not the monastic life just to be intellectualizing things and idealizing and "just thinking." It's living and experiencing the presence of the others in myself because they are part of me. Yes. You see? It's a question not of just, "I'm closing my eyes to the world." I *must know* what is happening. You have to be aware about all these things because the world is part of me. I can never leave the world.

I'm a monk so that God can fill me with His love and understanding to help others. That's how I understand and perceive monastic life, and only in that sense does it *make* sense. Otherwise I'm individualistic here, and that is not love. Love by nature is to reach out to the other and be concerned for the good of the earth, you see?

The *Rule of St. Benedict* says, "Prefer nothing to Christ." Christ says He is the Life and the Way and the Truth. If I'm being honest to myself — sincerely and truly — I must take all the human beings into consideration and become part of me and I part of them.

When I'm dealing with God I let him do what He wants with me. My attitude is that He has done so many good things which I see in my life. Now, my way of praying is basically thanksgiving. When I see all the good He has given me, I say, "Thank you God." My way is not asking for this or that. What I might ask for is one thing, to love. That's the best thing I know. If I can respect you as you are, and try to work for your completion, that's what I may ask: loving you, loving myself and everybody else. I want you — *and* Hitler — to be as happy as I will be. That's my greatest desire. If I will be so happy, I want each man to be experiencing the same. That's the fullness of my happiness. So my relationship with God is just simple.

My perseverance does not depend on me. It's a gift of God. You can think, "I'm a monk and I'm greater than the people in the world." No! God knows how He's going to save that person and knows how He's saving me, you see? That has nothing to do with whether or not for some reason I spend life drinking and womanizing and such. One can convert at the last moment and you go to the same place as me, and I have no problem with that. Look at the cross of Jesus, there were two thieves. One of them told him, "Please remember me in Your Kingdom." Jesus said, "Yes, you are going to be with me."

I came here in November 1989, and I've been happy since then. The brothers love me so much and I love them. I'm happy to be *here*, and another person would be happy to be *there*, and God is saving all people. Yeah! Sure!

✝   ✝   ✝

Brother Paul Bernard

Entered Gethsemani - February, 1955

I have always been interested in music, and although the chanting of the monks was pretty far afield from the classic Top 40 I was listening to in the sixties, I nonetheless was very intrigued by the monks' music.

Brother Paul Bernard was the abbey cantor in 1967 when I first met him. The cantor is in charge of all the music sung in church, and during the sixties Brother Paul wrote a lot of music that was used in the monks' choir, and is still being used today at New Clairvaux and other Trappist monasteries. It was because of Paul that my friend Joe and I played the Beatles' "Here Comes the Sun" in church that morning, and also through him that I was first acquainted with the Psalms as a living prayer.

An easygoing, gentle man with a generous smile and a powerful "bear hug," we became instant friends, and have remained so to this very day. As Joe and I would wander around the monastic grounds, we'd always pop into the abbey office to talk with Paul.

Currently he acts as choirmaster as well as cellarer, the latter being one of the most incredibly demanding jobs in the monastery aside from the abbot. With acres of prune and walnut orchards to manage and buy supplies for, he has to stay abreast with the newest farming procedures and equipment, and make decisions as to what the monastery should purchase for increased productivity. The position obviously requires a great deal of interaction with the outside world.

Between work periods, he swaps a seat at his computer for one behind the church organ, where he can be found accompanying the monks in their musical prayer to God.

I was in college at Columbia in New York. Thomas Merton went to Columbia, and in the bookstore there just happened to be a copy of his autobiography, *The Seven Storey Mountain*, and that was my first introduction to Cistercian life. I also bought his *The Waters of Siloe*, which is more specifically on Cistercian life, how it started and the his-

135

tory of it, and how it's come up to the present time. And what happened was, I became a Catholic and was baptized between my freshman and sophomore years in college on June 11, 1949.

The whole thing of the conversion — to go back to where I put it as the beginning in Fort Worth, Texas — we were all Protestant background and had no Catholics in our family. Of the many girls that I went with in high school, only one of them was a Catholic, and we dated pretty steadily during my senior year. We didn't talk much about Catholic religion, but that was my first, and as far as I know, my only contact with the Catholics. So anyway, this girl some way or another got me interested in Catholicism, and then in my first year in college I happened to see an advertisement in a magazine from the Vincentian Fathers for non-Catholics who were interested in the Catholic religion. They were out of St. Louis. So I wrote in and started a correspondence course on Catholicism with a Vincentian priest. And it turns out that the guy happened to be a Fort Worth man who was also a convert! So he made arrangements for me to meet the monsignor who had baptized him, when I went back to Fort Worth during the summer. By the time I got back there in summer it was all arranged, and I got baptized. I had completed the course and apparently it was enough instruction to be baptized.

Part of the required courses at Columbia were what they call humanities: literature, art, music, and one of the things that we had to listen to as part of this class was Gregorian chant. So it just . . . . I don't know, it just really knocked me off my feet! It was such a different type of music than anything I'd experienced before, and being a sort of musician myself, I guess God works with what we are. So from the very beginning I was attracted because of the Merton books, and I was listening to Gregorian chant. I knew Gregorian chant was sung in the monastery, and my whole attraction was not merely to Catholicism but to monasticism, and really, to Cistercianism as the most specific thing. I was very attracted to something other than just the regular parish life.

I was baptized between my freshman and sophomore year, and then that following Thanksgiving I made a retreat at Valley Falls, which was a monastery of our Order in Rhode Island. I was fascinated but scared. I said, "Boy, there was no way I could take this!" It was in the middle of winter, and of course that was back in the time when everything was all silent, and it was very forbidding. It was one of those things where you're fascinated but you're afraid, like in that book, *The Idea of the Holy*, by Rudolf Otto. It's the same sort of thing where he analyzes the human relationship with God as both fascination *and* fear. So it was the same thing that I was experiencing with Cistercian life. No way could I do

that! So that's kinda how I got into the Carmelites, as a sort of less austere and strict kind of life. I sort of made a detour. I finished my sophomore year at Columbia and then I entered the Carmelites on August 22,
1950.

The thing I remember most at the Carmelites was obedience, and particularly the novice master I had [laughing]. I don't know, he just seemed
to do everything he could to go contrary to what I wanted. Oh boy! I'll
tell you, I hated his guts [laughing]! One of the archaic things that we
had to do, whenever the novices walked by his room, you were supposed
to genuflect — just walking by his room! That was an old tradition in
the Carmelites [laughing]. Well, I just couldn't stand the guy, you know,
and I was walking by without genuflecting, and one day he caught me
and made me kneel down out there for — I don't know, four hours I
think it was — just kneeling right there at his door. I would say, *that* for
me was the hardest.

Most all religious have poverty, chastity and obedience. Those are the
main vows, and then we Cistercians have two others besides: stability
and conversion of manners. So the whole obedience thing where you
turn your life over, like Benedict says, something to the effect that a
monk does not have a body or his will as his own; it's turned over to
human superiors who are representing God. Well of course, obviously
that's a very deep sort of discipline, and I would say the *deepest* one where
you're giving up your freedom. But it's a discipline to help you give up
your ego; your own selfishness and things like that. And of course, the
more ego you've got, I guess the harder it is. That's the thing that's
behind it, to give up "self"; to become selfless. And you know, if you stick
with it, it works. It certainly becomes easier the more you do it. And I
think if you really give yourself to it, it does begin to strip you of your
own preferences and ego.

In my third or fourth year in the Carmelites, I asked to leave and go
back to secular life. Carmel wasn't my original attraction, and it just did-
n't have that much of a hold on me. I went and re-enrolled at Columbia,
got an apartment, and I was going to complete my college education. But
within a month or so I said, "Gee, this is not it." I think it was just kind
of a matter of things pulling in opposite directions, and I guess a lot of it
too, was my father, because I remember telling dad I want to get out; I
wanna have a whole bunch of kids [laughing]. I really wanted to get married and have kids.

So I asked to go to visit the novice master in Brookline,
Massachusetts. I'd heard about him some way or another, so I wrote him
and asked if I could talk it over. After talking it over with him I said,
"Gee, I'm gonna have to write the Carmelites back down in Texas and

say I'd really like to come back." So I wrote, and they said, "Okay come back," and I stayed another two years.

But my original love was Cîteaux. So very often we refer to our Order as Cîteaux. *Cistercium* is the Latin pronunciation, Cîteaux is the French. So my first love was Cîteaux, and since it looked too hard, I looked around for something sort of similar but not quite so hard [laughing]. I took Carmel as a kind of a second best, but I just couldn't get it out of my mind that I really liked this other life [Cistercian] better.

I had a friend that I'd met while I was in Columbia, an older woman,

Brother Paul on the community picnic in 1969.

and we corresponded, and I was telling her that I was still thinking about joining the Cistercians. She had an uncle over in the monastery of Melleray in France. Melleray is the mother house of Gethsemani. And without telling me she wrote to him. This guy told the French abbot of Melleray about me, that there's this Carmelite in Texas who's thinking about becoming Cistercian. So that abbot wrote to Father Louis [Thomas Merton] of all people, and told him about me, and even gave him my address! And without even knowing that all of this was going on, all of a sudden I got a letter from Thomas Merton, my hero [laughing]; a two-page letter explaining that he had heard from this French abbot that I wanted to become a Cistercian. The French abbot some way or another got the idea I wanted to come to France to be Cistercian, and he [Merton] said I should join in the United States.

So Father Louis went through all the American monasteries at that time, giving just a little bit of description of each one. He ended up saying, "Why don't you come to Gethsemani? We have the Holy Spirit here." So in February of '55 I went to Gethsemani. Then shortly afterward they made *this* foundation, the group that came out here. I think they left there in June of '55.

Gethsemani — when I first went out there — was a real honeymoon, you know, 'cause it was what I had been wanting for so many years. But the problem with Gethsemani at that time, there were over two hundred and thirty-five monks there, and it was so large. In addition to that, you only saw the abbot privately about twice a year because he had two hundred and thirty-five monks to see and five daughter houses to visit plus other things that abbots leave the monastery for. I was there for two years and I liked it. In fact, of all the places that I've ever lived, Gethsemani is still the place that comes up in my dreams more than any other place. It's really strange. But you know, some way or another it was an archetypical sort of place for me, which would sort of explain why I had such a gut attraction to the Cistercians.

The Carmelites were never as satisfying as Gethsemani, or you know, the Cistercian thing. I just never was quite happy there. Say you had a first love, and for some reason or another you couldn't marry her, and you married someone else [laughing]. Then you just weren't happy with *her*. All of a sudden your first love became available, you proposed, and she said "yes," so you go on a honeymoon and it's just real ecstasy!

Gethsemani stayed that way maybe about a year, then I guess the bigness of the place began getting to me. It was just too much like a big business or something, so that's when I began to say, "Well, I could go to a smaller monastery," so I asked to come here and I really loved it here, you know.

My family wasn't Catholic and they couldn't see it [monasticism] at all [laughing]! It just totally mystified them. I remember trying to explain it to my mother once. I used the word "absolute," you know: "The Absolute." For some reason I remember that I'd used that *particular* word. There was something that really fascinated me about "The Absolute," and wanting to give myself to that: to God. I don't know exactly how you explain that, but there was a real attraction to give my life to "The Absolute" rather than any particular ministry, like some people might join an order to teach or to work in a hospital or to work with poor people. Well, that didn't attract me. I saw Cistercian life as being *precisely focused* on God. We don't have a ministry.

Mother, I think, understood more than Dad did. They were both very good people, but I think to the very end my father could not understand. He loved my mom so much, you know, and they had such a good family and marriage that he just saw the beauty and value in marriage. His main thing was, of course, the fact that I would never be free to come home again, and that wasn't true in the Carmelites. You *could* go home, and I *did* go home. But once I entered Gethsemani, as far as I knew, I would never go home again. As far as *they* knew I would never go home again, and they could only visit me once a year for two or three days. I could only write them four times a year, and I could only receive mail from them four times a year.

For me, at least, the whole process of conversion to Catholicism and to Cistercianism is pretty much one continual dynamism. It was almost as if one just followed right after the other. Well see, back in those days, you were supposed to be a Catholic for three years before you entered a religious order. So when I entered the Carmelites I had to get a special indult; they had to go to Rome to get a permit for me to enter at such an early time after conversion. But that's why I say, it was all pretty much one dynamism.

I guess you'd just have to say the whole Cistercian game was something I liked even before I became a Catholic. And it was a game that I wanted to play for the rest of my life, because there's just hardly anything in Cistercianism that I *don't* like! But for me now, this also has a very human side. I guess the older I become, the more I feel that for a human being to give her or his life to God, that it's not done in a vacuum; it's done in a real sense as part of the human race and *for* the human race. So for a person to do that is in some unknown way helping the human race to become a better people.

One of the things I *don't* like is when somebody puts monks on a higher plane than other people. It's just different, is all that I can say — it's a different life — it's playing a different game in a certain sense. We're all playing the human game, but there's the monastic game, the Cistercian game, and then there's the married game or just living as a single person. We're just playing different games.

My relationship with God evolves just like a personal relationship does, and I guess for most of us, because of our Christian religion, it's centered on Jesus, a theandric being. Obviously we don't have any *physical* relationship with Him now [outside the Eucharist], but still He's a very real, living person. So one of the things that kind of a relationship does,

At the huller, walnuts are stripped of their outer skin and processed into large bins of clean, golden nuts. Brother Paul is sorting out damaged shells to insure a quality product during the 1975 harvest.

for me at least, it opens you up to something beyond space and time, and it's something where you have to move out of space and time because He's beyond time and space. It's hard to put into words; words are just not made for that kind of stuff, I guess. You can sort of stumble around [laughing].

I don't get any voices [laughing] and I don't hear things, and I don't see things, so you don't get confirmed that way. We speak quite a bit about a process of discernment. In other words, you kind of have to look around at your whole living situation; you have to look at other people, you have to look at the tradition. This is another whole big aspect, too, that has really been growing on me more and more in the last few years; the whole thing of Christian revelation, of God revealing Himself to His creation and the fact that the story is told *mainly* in the Scriptures, that it *has* been written down. But there's more than that. I mean, the Scriptures are just pointing to the whole "salvation history" and the romance between God and the human race. So calling all of that *tradition*, I use the Greek word which comes out of the New Testament, the *paradosis,* or the "handing on." So it's God revealing Himself to the human race, and then this being handed down through the Jewish people up until Jesus, and then moving out into the non-Jewish world. There's a lot of really concrete stuff in the Scriptures and in the whole tradition.

Tradition is just a translation of *paradosis.* Again, this is stuff that's kinda hard to talk about. There's this whole phenomenon of revelation being made *from* God *to* human beings, and then handed on from one generation to another. To me that is just . . . . You know, it kinda blows my mind! In addition to the tradition, to get down to specifics, you then begin looking around the human environment, you talk to people. So to me, one of the big things is the human relations of the people you're living with. You check things out with them. And then of course, one of the big parts of our tradition is the abbot himself who takes the place of Christ. So you check it out with him, and you've got a spiritual director and you've got friends; you've got all your brothers to check things out with.

I did have one experience where I heard . . . . I didn't hear it physically, but I heard a very beautiful song. It was just a phrase. For years I couldn't even say it to anybody else because I'd get so choked up with it, you know, and tears would come down. But it was "Come Little Children, Dance with Me." And it came out in music. I can't sing it for you because even now I would get choked up if I did. But I felt *that* was God talking to the human race: "Come Little Children, Dance with Me." And if you think about that, that is so beautiful — "Dance with Me" — and "Little Children." I thought of people dying and they're going to dance with God, you know. Wow!

I don't remember the date, but I remember where I was; it came when I was walking out on the south road by the old apricot trees that are long gone. And as I said, boy, I just cried and cried and cried! And every time I would sing it I would cry, you know, and I just couldn't tell anybody that until several years later. I've told very few people, really.

I've looked into quite a few of the Eastern religions. Zen, I guess mostly, but also the Tibetans, because of the fact that we had several Tibetan monks visit here. I really like that Zen thing, about reality is in the here and now, so that eternity is right here and now. It's not something you go off into a Never Never Land, but it's *here!* See, I just feel that there's

Previously the cantor for many years, Paul is now the choir master who plays organ for all church offices and services.

a lot of paths to God, and I feel that the most secular person can arrive — even though he goes through this life without a lot of spiritual awareness or a lot of spiritual striving — that he can become just as close to God as we can, and maybe closer because you can goof it up in here just as well, you know, like the parable of the talents. You could receive all of this wonderful stuff and then go bury it, not make anything out of it. Whereas somebody out there [in the world] that has received just a tiny little bit, and yet they can make everything out of it through God. Because it's not just — as far as I'm concerned, and that's, I think, the way the church teaches, too — it's not just what *we* do, it's also the gift that we're given from God, and God can choose whoever He wants.

Myself, I would never be able to live as a hermit, I don't think. I appreciate the community. *Appreciate* it? I *love* it! To me, that's one of the big things about Cistercianism, it's very much community. Balance is one way to put it, and it's also seeing and experiencing "The Absolute" in your brother and you. It's not as if I'm gonna go off and be alone, and close my eyes and shut my ears and experience "The Absolute" [laughing]. I experience it right *here and now*. We're just as close to Him now as I would be in church. So yeah, you don't want to box it up and say, "Well now, when I go to church I pray, and I'm getting in touch with God." No! He's as close here as He is there.

I suppose a lot of people come into a monastery thinking — I guess maybe I did, too — "The only time I'm really close to God is when I'm in church or when I'm in meditation." I would say that was my experience at first. I don't feel that way anymore. That has *really* changed [laughing]. I spend a lot of time working, because of my position as business manager, it's surprising how much time it takes, and if I had the notion that this is time taken away from God, or from the important things, I would really be under tension and stress.

I think we are free of a lot of the stresses other people have, or people who are in different types of life. But I think every lifestyle has its own type of stress. Like the stress that I mentioned about obedience. Well, I don't think that'll ever go away. Then there's creative tension, you know, good stress.

I can understand why people see us as copping out. I don't necessarily try to defend that. My father didn't use the words "copping out" — that just wasn't part of his vocabulary — but that's what he was thinking; throwing my life away, no productivity, not contributing to the beauty and goodness of the world in a *real* way. In a sense, people are coming from different worlds — different mind sets, different faith systems, different belief systems — not necessarily just religious systems but philosophical positions. And since you're talking different languages, you don't really need to defend yourself or feel called to defend yourself. You just *be!* And if you have a different life mode like we do, well, we could question a lot of people out there: "What the hell are *you* doing with your life?" You know [laughing]?

And as I say, this business of being a monk not just for yourself but for the human race . . . . I know a lot of people don't understand that, it just doesn't mean anything to them. Well, it does mean something to *me*. I

As cellarer (business manager) of the farming operations, much of Paul's time is spent at his desk in front of a computer.

feel that it's very real, and therefore I just feel very close to the human race, you know? And I feel growing closer and closer as I get older, even with people who have died. That was one of the things when my folks died, I really experienced that I got closer to them after they died. I started praying for them and other people who had died. And I still do it, you know. I say the rosary and I mention them by name at the end of every decade. I also pray the psalter continually, five songs every day, and it's a very archetypal experience.

The Psalms are very, very *human,* and I know some people in years

Paul streaks across the grounds under the watchful eye of the now-dismantled water tower.

past have told me they don't mean very much to them. But see, they're the bulk of our prayer that we say as a community, but I have gotten into saying them *myself*. Anyway, what I'm getting at is this whole business of life being lived in more than the here and now, that you have a connection with people who have died. Many of my prayers I say specifically for all who *have* lived, who *are* living, who *will* live. You know, some way or another, even with the people who have not yet been born I feel a real close relationship. So that being the case, and the fact that I'm giving myself to God, as it were, *for* these people, to me that justifies the life that I've chosen or have been chosen for.

It won't work here if you're escaping or if you're trying to flee from something. In a sense you *are*, because we do speak of that. I mean, that's part of the tradition in monasticism when we speak of the *fuga mundi*; the flight from the world. That's one of the things that defines the monk; he flees from the world. But it can't be just negative, that you're fed up with the world and you're trying to get away from this thing that you're fed up with. Don't escape! There's gotta be some real positive attraction too, because if there's not, it just ain't gonna work.

I'm fairly much at peace with myself. I'm happy with my job, even though it takes a heck of a lot of time. I'm happy to be here, doing what I'm doing.

✝   ✝   ✝

Brother John Cullen

Entered New Clairvaux - 1962

Brother John Cullen was one of the guest masters during my initial visit to the monastery. To a kid suddenly finding himself in the company of thirty-five monks and away from home for the first time, it's only natural to gravitate to those personalities who seemed the most outgoing. John Cullen was one of them.

Because my friend Joe and I were always laughing and happy, it seemed to bring out John Cullen's sense of fun and his wry humor. In later years, when Joe and I would come up together for a retreat, or if I came alone, John Cullen always made a special effort to drop by our room to find out what we'd been doing with our lives. Conversation ran the gamut from spirituality to the theater and old Hollywood films.

Life has come full circle in the past thirty years, for when I was making many trips to Vina in preparation for this book, John Cullen had once again become guest master. And as in days past, we can still be found sitting in one of the old rooms in St. John, discussing the latest book he's read, or perhaps debating Cary Grant's best performances. Such are the moments I will always treasure, and Brother John Cullen has been a dear friend over the years.

I worked for a lithograph company in San Francisco. At the time I left there I was a plate maker, but I started out as a color proofer, and I had been doing that until I went in the army in '51. So I'd been in that for three years, and then I finished my apprenticeship in the other department as a plate maker, mostly advertising, labels and things like that.

Like so many other people, I'd read *The Seven Storey Mountain*, and I think that influenced me considerably. When I was a little kid I thought about becoming a missionary but didn't give it any serious thought. I also knew that there was an Order — what they were called I didn't know —

but they were kind of strict and they didn't talk much, and maybe didn't eat meat. I don't remember very much about it. And I thought, "Well, that sounds pretty good, too." But like I say, until I was a young adult I never thought anything serious about this kind of life.

I was doing a lot of reading and going to Mass, and I had a spiritual director who was a Jesuit. I guess you could say I had a conversion before this, and that's what led to the reading and the spiritual direction toward a more serious consideration of what I was going to do with my life. I wasn't converted from any way of *sinful* life, in a sense of wrong doing. No, I was always a Catholic, and I suppose I maybe questioned it at one time or another and resolved whatever doubts I may have had. Not that they were doubts, but you know, I gave it some "Why am I Catholic?" — that sort of thing. And there was no problem, but I did give things more serious thought.

I think when I was a senior in high school I began going to Mass in the morning. Not necessarily daily Mass, but quite often I'd go before going to school. Then I went to work and kind of drifted away from that part of it, and began going again when I was nineteen or twenty. By the time I was twenty-one I had a pretty fair idea of what I wanted to do, and that was to become a Trappist. Nothing else ever had the slightest appeal for me. As a youngster, I knew of their existence and I knew too, that they were in Ireland, because they had a school there, Mount Melleray. But there were a lot of things going on at the time, and it didn't seem feasible, and I thought, "I'll wait, and if it's the right thing for me, it'll eventually develop."

I went into the army, came out in '53 and went up to Holy Trinity [Trappist Monastery] in Utah. I kind of liked what I saw, and I went back again in August or early September of '55 for probably a week. I didn't know it at the time, but *this* place [New Clairvaux] had been founded in July of '55, and I came up here, oh, in '56, I think. I was on a vacation and I had friends in Sacramento who knew about the place, and I asked them where it was and how I'd find it. I was going up to Redding to visit a friend of mine who was living up there and I drove in and looked around. Wasn't terribly impressed with the place. You know, I wasn't thinking of it; I wasn't giving it any thought, really.

I remember I met Father Anselm, who was the superior then, and he showed me around. We had a nice talk, and I said, "When I come back from Redding, can I stop by and spend the night?" He said, "Yeah, sure." I stayed the night, and there was a solemn profession going on the next day and I was here for that. *Still* wasn't impressed with the place!

I didn't come back again until '61, after I'd been to Europe. I got a little more impressed with the place but I was going to go to Trinity in

150

Utah again for a weekend, and for some reason I can't think of why now, I decided not to. I was going to fly up and rent a car or something like that. I didn't want to drive the whole thing. Then I asked a few questions here, and got the answers that I guess I needed, and forgot all about Utah. I spoke to the abbot. We talked about it and he said, "If you want to enter you can come up here in May next year," and that's what I did. That would have been '62. Been here ever since.

I don't know, something happened when I came here for the weekend. Whether I just decided that it was more reasonable to enter in a place that was closer to San Francisco, or whether some of the people impressed me . . . . You remember Giacomo? Probably not. Yeah, well if you saw him you'd remember! I met him, and I think John Paul was here, certainly. He was guest master. And let's see, who else? That's about all I met, and things kind of just fell into place.

I guess I wasn't really satisfied out there [in society]. I had the idea that whatever I had wasn't really enough for me; it wasn't enough to satisfy or to fulfill me. I'd thought about getting married. I was dating a very nice girl. Still hear from her. In fact, today I was thinking she owes me a letter. But I wasn't, well, I wasn't satisfied, and I didn't think I ever . . . . You know, when I was younger I figured by the time I'm twenty-four I'd be married and start raising a family. But as I say, when I was twenty to twenty-one, I had *this* idea, and I kinda kept it in my mind for the future. There were other things.

My dad was ill, and my brother wasn't doing so well. I won't say they needed me at home, but I was of some — not necessarily financial support but I was of some support at home. Eventually I realized as I got older that there will always be something that'll keep you [from entering] one way or the other, you know? And I thought, "I'm just going to have to make a decision. I can't just sit on the fence all my life." So that's what I did. I was under simple vows from '64 until 1970, for six years, and then I made my solemn vows. There were ten in the novitiate when I entered, between choir novices and brother novices, and I was number eleven, but they're all gone. All kinds of people left in the sixties.

I didn't have any problems at all as far as being disappointed. I don't ever remember being disillusioned. Let's see, I entered in May and my aunt died in June — June thirteenth — so that would have been about less than a month after I entered. And I felt badly about that because I was very fond of her, and the hot weather had come and I developed a heat rash. I went to bed one night and I thought, "Well, I've had it! Tomorrow morning I'll just turn over when the bell rings, get up later in the morning, go down and tell the abbot I've tried and I'll just go back to San Francisco." And this is what I was thinking when the bell rang in

Pruning pole slung over his shoulder, John Cullen walks an orchard road on a crisp, clear day in 1968.

the morning. But I got up, got dressed and went where I was supposed to go, and had no more thought of leaving — never had any misgivings or doubts. I didn't have any highfalutin or high flown expectations about who I was gonna meet or what the life was gonna be like. I had a pretty fair idea of what it was gonna be like, and I don't think I was ever surprised by anything that happened. I kinda took things in stride. I'm not a worrier, or I'm certainly not a "Type A" person [laughing]. I'll be very surprised if I go with a heart attack, at least at a relatively young age!

When I came there was more silence. Yes, although you could always get permission to speak to whoever you wanted to speak to. Then when they gradually eased up on that, it was a matter of you have permission to talk during work but *only* about work. Then gradually it just seemed to slip. I think it was probably a psychological need. I remember Brother Elias was asking me something, and I suppose now that I think of it I was probably very rude. He was talking to me, asking me questions, and I was answering him by signs, and he said, "What the hell's the matter with you? Can't you talk?" And I said, "Yes, of course I can talk!" This was before we had general speaking when we could talk about work. I'm not even sure that at this particular time that we *could* talk about work. There were some people who would make signs, but they would whisper along with their signs so that you certainly knew what they were saying. But the signs could be very easily misunderstood. I had an incident one day . . . . I was out working with one of the novices, and I was making signs to him, and he got quite angry. Whether he just couldn't understand my signs or what, but I could tell.

It's not the same sign language as deaf people use but it's very similar. Ours were kind of minimal, so you couldn't say everything with signs. That's why you'd whisper. It could be very frustrating. Some people just didn't like signs.

The Discipline

Contained within the Regulations of the Order of Cistercians of the Strict Observance, printed in 1926, there is a paragraph on page 173 under the heading "Penances" titled **The Discipline.** This practice was followed into the 1960's until abolished as part of a spirit of renewal in the Order. The passage states as follows:

*To perform this penance we use an instrument commonly called a **Discipline.** It consists of a lash of five small cords, each having five knots. The discipline is taken on the shoulders. This penance is performed in the dormitory every Friday of the year, immediately after the Night Office, for the space of a **Miserere,** except from Christmas to the 13th of January inclusively, during Paschal time, and when a Feast of Sermon occurs. The discipline is kept out of sight under the mattress or pillow.*

The other day a man gave a talk about a lay brother in Villers named Arnulf, and he used to beat himself mercilessly, and he actually enjoyed it. This was back in the Twelfth or Thirteenth century, and he would laugh, and he was getting a certain satisfaction out of all this. He would say, "This is for so and so's needs, and this is for somebody elses' needs," or that sort of thing. He was very good about helping other people, and I guess he lived in a community, but he would go off by himself into his little cell or whatever, to do this. He had permission to do this on the condition that if anybody would need him for spiritual direction or anything, that he would come out and deal with them. He went to his reward, God bless him! And all the time during this talk I was thinking, "Well, this poor man was really wacko!" I listened politely, and I laughed when something was amusing, but it certainly didn't have any appeal for me whatever.

We were still doing it [the discipline] in '67 when I was the guest-master here. Oh yeah. It was only on Friday mornings. I mean, it wasn't any prolonged thing; it was supposed to be the space of an Our Father or something. See, we had cells, and everybody was in a cell, and somebody gave a signal and you started, and then they gave a signal and you stopped. It was a monastic practice. Everybody did it. Oh yes! And it wasn't a punishment as such. It was just a matter of . . . . well, they called it "the discipline." Whether it was a question of self-discipline . . . . I'm not into that sort of thing, actually, at all.

Yes, in fact, I was just telling one of the novices the other day, when I entered it was this time of year — it was after Easter — and they didn't do it during Eastertide. It was after Pentecost, I guess, when they resumed it. Whatever time it was, Father Joseph was the novice master. He said, "Well, Friday we resume the discipline. I suppose you're curious to know how it's done?" And I said, "No, not particularly." And I wasn't at all [laughing]! I couldn't see it — I still don't see it.

I try to keep somewhat abreast of what's going on. It's much easier for us now than it was in past years. Looking back, I can honestly say that I didn't know anything about the Vietnam war. I mean, I knew there was a war but . . . . well, I don't know that there was that much information available. The abbot kept kind of a strict lid on things. Things loosened up in '68, and since then things have changed considerably.

I don't think I'm inclined to be a hermit. No, I need company. I'm a very reserved person, and you might even say a private person. But I mean, I need people and social contact. I don't like to be overly friendly with people, and sometimes I'll find myself saying, "Gee, why doesn't this guy let up and go away, and do something so I can be alone and do my work," or "I hope he's not gonna stop and talk to me when he passes me, because I don't really have anything to say to him," that sort of thing. So in that sense, I don't go out of my way to be friendly here in the monastery, but I need contacts.

Some people are very sensitive, and you have to be careful of what you say and how you say it, and what you do. *Oh, you have to be careful!* Some people are very easily offended. I don't think I am, but I know we've had people in the past . . . . I can think of someone who's no longer here, and well, he didn't stay — he couldn't stay, I guess. You never knew what to do, what to say when he was around. He would just be offended by the least little thing that you'd say or do, and you can't go through life like that. Nobody can go through life like that, especially when you're living in such close quarters.

See, one thing about living outside. If you've got a job, it's five days a week or whatever it might be — from nine to five — and around five you turn off the light and close the door, and for the most part you can forget about it. But we can't do that, because we're bumping into each other continuously throughout the day, and you have to be a little bit careful about peoples' feelings. And we're not always careful, you know. Sometimes we don't think about what we say before we say it. But in general we get along.

I'd have to say I don't think we're any different from any other "single person" in the world. I mean, we don't have a wife and we don't have a family, but we're making our own way; we're earning our living, and theoretically, we're contributing to society in some way. We're just single like other people outside that are single. We have a different lifestyle, that's the only difference that I can see.

Sometimes I wonder if I'm making any progress at all [laughing]. I *really do* wonder. You have to take stock every once in awhile and realize, you know, "What am I doing?" or "What am I doing with my time? Am I getting where I expect to be, or where I hope to be? Am I getting out of the life what I want? Am I putting enough into the life?" You do have to take stock.

I remember my pastor in San Francisco had told me, he said, "You'll never see any results of your life while you're there. Whatever you do, you'll never have anything concrete to show for it in the sense that you won't be a success." And I've often thought of that, and it was very true. You need to do what you can, but you'll never know. How do you measure how successful you are? You can't, as far as I'm concerned. You just hope that you're doing the right thing, and that what you're doing is what you're supposed to be doing.

I've often thought that I felt closer to God through my prayer life and my reading outside before I came than I ever have here, which is kind of a strange thing to say, I guess. Now, that could have been just wishful thinking, you know. I won't say self-deception, but it could be that it was

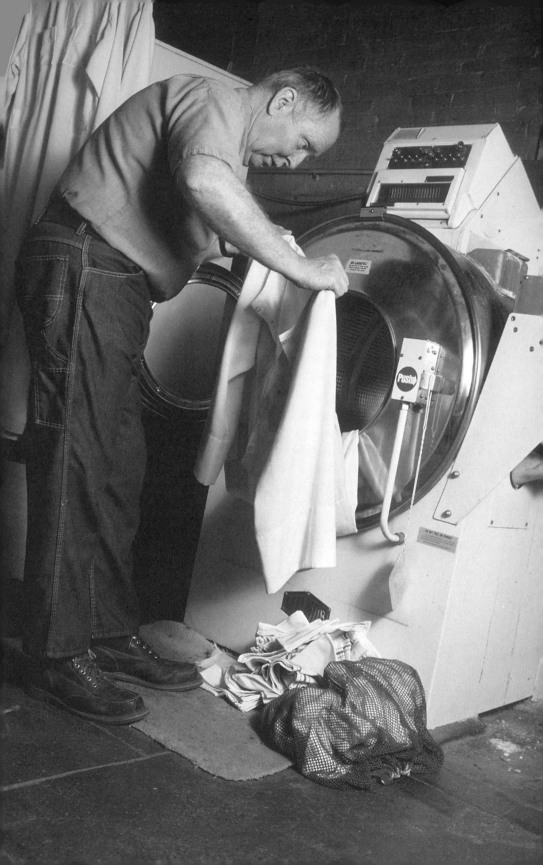

Laundry detail! Washing, drying and pressing all those habits along with work clothes and linens is a full time job.

just that I felt that way. It's funny that I say that, because outside I was not satisfied that I was where I wanted to be or where I should be, whereas here, I feel very comfortable and satisfied that I am where I should be. I think maybe that shows that I'm still progressing without actually attaining anything. I certainly haven't attained any mystical heights. I don't *think* I have, anyway [laughing]. I'd be very surprised.

We had a fella — he was a Greyhound bus driver, and this was when I was going to San Francisco occasionally — he would come up here and he knew that I was going to San Francisco. And he asked me one day — he had ideas of intrigue here — he said, "Doesn't it bother you that you have to leave the monastery and go to San Francisco?"

I said, "It's something that I'm doing, you know, that I'm asked to do. I don't have an obligation, but I'm helping my mother out, and it doesn't bother me to go to San Francisco and see people and read newspapers and things like that. When I'm there, I watch television or go out for a meal. That doesn't bother me in the least." And he couldn't understand it. In all the years that I was going there — and I started when my brother died in '69 — I got along fine. I had no trouble living in the city at all; going shopping or doing whatever I had to do. I did feel, though, I was actually quite depressed by that situation. And looking back now, there were a lot of things that I did not do; a lot of people that I didn't look up and places that I didn't go because I just felt that I couldn't enjoy it, and I didn't want to impose myself with this mental attitude on someone else. But other than that I managed quite well.

I've grown in being here thirty-six years. I see things differently now, where my expectations are different than they were when I entered. Not that I've been disappointed or disillusioned in anything, it's just that I have a different viewpoint. I don't know if what I'm saying makes any sense at all, but it's an ongoing thing. That's about all I can say. You can't define it. It's not like you were getting a report card or something, or you were getting a measure of your progress. We have the spiritual director and the confessor, and you pretty much know that you're doing the right thing; that you're heading in the right direction. Maybe you're not always putting as much effort into it as you could, and that's where you need someone to direct you, to help you along.

I would say we develop a capacity as we go through life for whatever lies ahead, an openness, and if you're open to the ultimate that God will give you — whatever that might be — *that's* what you will receive and recognize. Whereas, if you have no capacity at all, or very limited or minimal capacity, then that's what you'll get. If your expectations are low, that's what you'll get, but you won't be any less satisfied because your expectations *were* low. If you have just a little capacity for what-

Brother John Cullen gets caught in the abbot's headlights as he attempts a late night kitchen raid. Actually — always a good sport — he is posing as a model for a Hitchcockian version of the monastic life!

ever it's going to be, and you get that, well then, I'm sure you'll be satisfied.

Thursday when I was going in to town, I had Matthew Fox's book
Original Blessing with me, and Father Paul looked at the index — and if
there is a section on reincarnation I didn't get to it — but he said that
he's been asked by a nun to do a paper on reincarnation vs. resurrection.
And I said, "Well for me, resurrection is much easier to consider than
reincarnation." And I say that because I haven't experienced either one
of them [laughing]. But resurrection is part of our faith, whereas reincarnation is not. I'd be very surprised to find out that there is such a thing.
I have no personal experience of ever having been something from the
past. If I have been, why wouldn't I know about it? I — "The Person" —
me, myself!

I'd have to say that I often wonder about hell. I'd probably say I don't
believe in hell in a sense of eternal fire. If you deny God completely, you
know, if you just turn away from Him, well then that might be a hell of
your own making, you know. I have no idea what's in store for anybody
in the hereafter. Somebody like Hitler for instance. I have no idea where
he's gonna be. I just hope we're not in the same area, frankly!

There's always room for improvement, but I am at peace with myself.
I was just thinking this afternoon . . . . I don't know what put it in my
mind. Well, I'll tell ya, I *know* what put it in my mind: I had two skin
cancers removed Thursday — basal cell carcinomas — and that sounds
pretty grim, but I don't think it is. It could be serious if the doctor didn't
get it all. So I said, "When will you know?" And he said, "You come back
in ten days and I'll let you know." And I said, "What happens if you did-
n't get it all?" He said, "We'll cross that bridge when we come to it."

But there's nobody depending on me for anything. At least one quarter of my high school class is gone — possibly a third — and I thought,
"Well, *I'm* here. I'm sixty-two, and some of them didn't reach sixty. So,
you know, I'm not gonna live forever.

We had a New Year's party, and I forget what the question was —
maybe it was, "What was the most significant thing that happened to
you in the past year?" When my turn came to answer I said, "I've come
to terms with my own mortality. I've accepted the fact that I'm not going
to live forever, and I don't worry about it." We're not used to dying
[laughing]. We haven't had any personal experience of it. I think it just
dawned on me.

Brother John Cullen

To anyone thinking of entering, I'd say think it over very carefully. See as much of the world as you could, and then rethink it over very carefully and pray over it, and give it serious thought, not just because you happen to think that it's a romantic way of living or a rustic romance, as Father Joseph once called it many years ago when I was a novice. That's about all I'd say. I mean, you come, and if you don't like it, well, you're free to leave.

✝   ✝   ✝

Postscript: The doctor did get it all,
and Brother John Cullen
is as feisty as ever!

Abbot Thomas Davis

Entered at Gethsemani - 1951

Being abbot of a monastery is a difficult vocation. You relinquish the anonymity of the average monk to place yourself in a position that deals directly with "the world" on various levels. The abbot not only has the community as his spiritual responsibility, but also the financial well-being of the monastery. Not every monk is cutout to be an abbot, and those who are able to fulfill the requirements and perform them well are extremely valuable to the Order.

Abbot Thomas Davis was not the abbot when I first arrived at Vina, and although I did have a passing relationship with him, I didn't really get to know the man until many years later when he granted me permission to interview and photograph the monks.

Father Thomas is an extremely dedicated, caring individual who has the rare ability to sift through a problem or situation and assess it objectively. He has been a staunch supporter of this book project, with an open-mindedness and humor that has seen us both through some difficult decisions. I am deeply thankful for his respect and friendship.

In his interview, Father Thomas talks about the problems involved in running a monastery in today's society, and delves deep into his own soul to discuss his relationship with God, the community and his "self."

I was deciding after the eighth grade that I would go away to the seminary, with the intention of studying for the priesthood, to join the monastery St. Meinrad's in Indiana. In those days, there were a lot of vocations, and we had about five boys from our parish who were somewhere in the twelve-year program for the priesthood: high school, four years of college, and four years of theology. It was kinda the "in" thing to do, and I wanted to be a priest so I entered the monastery after high school at age seventeen.

It's rare if people persevere at that age. I don't recommend it, but I know three other abbots who entered young; one was eighteen, one was nineteen, and there was another that was about the same age. In fact, our former Abbot General was seventeen when he entered, so it's possible, but it's not something I would recommend. I never would take anyone that young, 'cause in some respects you don't know what you want at that age. It's amazing. Sometimes you *do* know, and of course, I didn't have the options forty years ago that people have today. You know, "What am I going to do with my life?" Now, with the jet age, you can jump on a plane and go up to Colorado and ski for the weekend. Well, in my day if you went to Colorado it was a lifetime trip, you know, for a little town hick. Today the world's at your feet. The Peace Corps hadn't come in, and none of that, so in some respects it would be a little harder to face yourself, because you've already got the parameters in which you *have* to face yourself.

I chose at an early age that I'm going to be a monk, and that meant I have to face myself as a monk. I didn't live a life and have other commitments, and then finally decide this is what I want to do. For example, people get married young or get married hastily, and decide to make a go of it. There's the same situation. You have to make your choices within a certain parameter. However, I think when it's all said and done, anger is not limited to any age, and everybody has to face their own inner anger somewhere along the line, or you end up being an angry person. And you can be an angry person in any walk of life, so I think the basic "facing of the self" is the same; it's just a question of when you're going to do it.

The problem is, if you decide to put yourself in the context of doing it at a young age, perhaps it's a little more difficult because either you end up realizing that you *have* these parameters, or you end up switching vocations or something. That's always a possibility — you never know. So I think that basically the spiritual life is staying put in the vocation you've chosen, and trying to put yourself together in that situation. And to me, age is kind of irrelevant, although there is a certain human maturity that has to take place; a certain level, anyway, to make decent choices, and I had to do that within the monastic context.

In grade school I very much felt a calling, not to the diocesan priesthood but to the monastic life, and in those days priesthood and monasticism were not separated as much as they are today. It was just you became a monk or you became a priest. It was different, and so I felt a calling. I knew I did not want to become a diocesan priest. I wanted very much to be a monk, 'cause I had, as a young child, been acquainted with monastic life. Not so much the Trappists but the Benedictines, and I was going toward the Benedictines. When I got to the seminary I found out about the Trappists, and they were even more contemplative and cloistered, and that was an appeal to me.

It's the contemplative dimension. I like that very much. I didn't care too much for the active life and teaching and so on. I don't think I could articulate it very well in those days. I just felt drawn, and I knew that I didn't want to be a diocesan priest because there was a lot of activity involved in running a parish, and it just didn't appeal to me. And then with the monastic life — the sense of community and also a type of spirituality — I felt that the monks had a more spiritual thrust perhaps than the diocesan priest had.

I entered as a monk at Gethsemani in 1951. Brother Adam was there, and Brother Casmir, and Father Timothy. I came to Vina [New Clairvaux] about 1955. The group came in July, and I came in September. I had been asked by Dom James [abbot of Gethsemani], about a week before they left, to come. I was one of the last ones to be asked, and I mean, I was terrified of the thought of going all the way to California! It was just too soon, and I said no: I didn't want to come. But you didn't tell Dom James no, you know, so I could have been with the original group but chose not to.

I left [New Clairvaux] in '66. I had asked to go away for a six-month absence, and I felt I just needed . . . . The community was unsettled, and something told me inside that I needed to get away; I needed a little space, like a sabbatical. So I asked the abbot and he agreed.

I became superior [of New Clairvaux] in '70, so I think it was a kind of preparation of God giving me a little distance from the community so I could kinda sort things out, and see what was going on here. And those were the times when a lot of things were changing in the country in the sixties. I remember the assassination of Martin Luther King and so on, and it was a real time of change. So I think it was a direct preparation. The abbot of Gethsemani was here, and the community decided not to proceed to elect the new abbot right away, so I was actually *appointed* in 1970. But in '72 — a year and a half later — we proceeded with a regular major election, and then I was elected.

The community can choose anybody they want [to be abbot], but one of the qualifications is you have to be a priest, and that still remains in the new constitutions. I don't know how that's going to work now that we have fewer priests, but you're elected by the community. It's only with the solemn professed, and it's a secret thing, and they have ballots and you write the name of the person you think should be abbot. They keep voting until they get somebody. It has to be simple majority: one over half would be a simple majority.

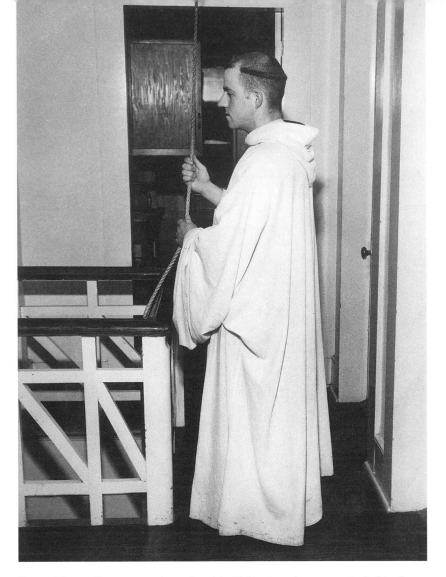

Frater Thomas Davis, a simple professed in 1956, rings the community bell in the old mansion, which burned to the ground in 1970. The contemporary looking hairstyle was called a "tonsure."

The abbot does set the tone of the community in many ways. I mean, he does personality-wise, and you can see that in our communities. Each community's different; that's just a fact, but at the same time it doesn't mean that he imposes things.

It's not so much *me* and *them*; it's just us all together. Well, it [being abbot] is hard. I don't know, I just . . . . [laughing] I think you have stress in terms of personal relationships. I'll use an analogy. When two people get married, you have to adjust to one another, and there is stress there at times. Well in a monastery, we have the same thing. Perhaps not quite as intense, because in some ways there's not that kind of intimacy, but at the same time you're living together all the time. However, I think the abbot and some other officials — like maybe the cellerer — we are in situations where we *do* have to always relate to people, and you *have to* relate, and that's hard. That's one of the stresses I think that perhaps an average monk wouldn't have. We all have it to a certain degree — of relating and communication and so on — but then you have the responsibility of keeping the whole thing viable like a supervisor at a big organization or company.

Our major sources of income are the prunes and walnuts. There's not that much of a surplus. I think it's the same as, you know, a farmer: one year you have a good crop, and the next year you don't have such a good crop. One year the price is up, and the next year it's not so good. We do well, but a lot of it has to be reinvested to upkeep the machinery, and we need to buy machinery these days. Fortunately we are able to support ourselves from the crops.

Then we have the daughter houses in Asia. We do some charity from time to time, so we have this kind of thing going on. We're getting some donations, and we do get donations from the guest house. Then over the years — the good years — there's been investments, and so we do have a small source from the investments, so all that pooled together makes it possible.

There's just a lot of business. The normal concerns of making sure work's going along all right, that the business is going ahead, things you've got to take care of, pressures that come in terms of maybe deadlines to meet like construction and so forth, correspondence, dealing with the formation, helping newcomers discern vocation or monks work through their own personal problems from time to time. If they come to you, you get involved in things the average monk wouldn't be involved in. And then there's what they call a triangular relationship, that you and I have trouble due to a third-party situation, or we try to get three things going here. It can be a person or it can be an issue and, you know, who's gonna win of these three? That kind of stuff goes on a lot.

Some people can take the tension and stress in work and some people can't. You have to be able to. You've got to! It gets you at times, but still . . . . Sometimes they can all come at once [laughing], and sometimes nothing happens, you know, you have days when it's quite peaceful.

I'm not too concerned about the world creeping in. My concern is that we use what the world offers us to express our basic values, and some-

Posing with Brother Odo Metten around 1956. Odo was a lay brother who died in 1978 from Lou Gehrig's disease.

times we have to take reactions against it.

You know, I don't know how I can articulate it, but the culture and the civilization — I mean, what goes on in the country — is always reflected some way in the community, because people come from around the country. I don't know if it penetrates, it's just this is where we come from; it's what we come in with. That's the formation, that's the postulant's way of thinking. The community just can't live in an isolation of the country. That does infiltrate. I don't know if that's the exact word, but it's the pressure of trying to keep it out. But the point is, that this is what's going on in the country and this is where you live, so that's what's going on in your life. You know, if there was a revolution in your city, your family would experience it whether you were part of it or not. It would have an effect on you, and that's what's happened with us.

See, in the old days before Vatican II, we definitely had a lot of structure. I think life in general had a lot of structure. It was the "flower children" who were rebelling so much. We had a lot of structure, and it wasn't a question so much of obeying or disobeying instruction. The abbot was there, in a way, to make sure that everything went smoothly — that people obeyed — and even the abbot didn't have as many decisions to make as the abbots today because we had our rules. You just follow the rules. Our whole life was detailed as to how we walked, where we walked, what we ate; the whole day was very detailed, and that all *went*, so that now the community can kind of determine its own way of life. So we have a real communal spirituality called the *common will*, which is quite Cistercian. It's not necessarily the same as consensus, but we get together, talk about issues, and set a direction, but the abbot's ultimately responsible.

I can't be constantly bucking the community. For example, suppose I think that this is the way something should be done, but I can see that the community decides it's going to be going this other way. Well now, part of my being selfless is to say, "Okay Thomas, back off now. You know this way it can work." It might be better but I won't admit it. Or maybe it won't be better but it *can* work, and since the community is kinda opting for this, okay, give it a try, go along with it. So that's how I keep in step with the community. It's rare, but now and then there might be situations where I will have to simply say no according to our basic monastic values, that I don't think that's the right direction to be going. Usually there's enough people in the community that see that.

Of course, you're gonna have people wantin' to do it and not wantin' to do it — and all shades in between — and somewhere along the line whatever the Holy Spirit wants us to do has to surface; it has to percolate to the top, and then the final decision is made. For the most part, the direction set by the community is valid. I don't think I've ever been in a situation where the community has opted to do something that was really not the proper thing to do.

So the community is involved in many more decisions than they ever had to worry about previously, because it's a different approach. At the same time, I don't want to give the impression that everything is a communal decision because it's not. It's not! We try to make a distinction between things that will affect everybody in a kind of personal way, then they have a chance to express their observations one way or another, if they want to. Some are quite content.

I should be careful — because somebody might disagree with me — but I never sensed in our particular community a real faction in a sense that some wanted to hold to the old and some with the new. I never sensed that at all. There might be degrees of how to do the new, but no, I never sensed that here with this group. That's been one of the blessings, and many religious communities have had that problem. Now, I'm not too sure why that happened. I think one reason is that our layout here is much different; the structure. We don't have the old traditional-type monastery — we have more the village-type — and your environment really affects your mentality. What you see *does* affect how you live, in a way, and I think also the fact that we had a lot of lay brothers. The choir monks were the minority, 'cause we were founded with a lot of lay brothers. Usually any split was down along the lines of the lay brothers and choir monks — but not always — and we never really had that kind of split because we really worked together.

And then another element that might have had something to do with it was the fact that we had a strong group who entered about the same age, and we've got an age group that was pretty much the same in those days. We didn't have a lot of older people that really wanted to hold on to the old way. We *were* the older people, so to speak, and that helped. There was more of a peer relationship in terms of age.

See, we have a spiritual tradition in the Cistercian Order, and we've got the whole monastic tradition of what a monk does as opposed to what, say, a married person would do. The point is getting in touch with our tradition, and not being caught up in a type of spirituality which is more *devotional*. I don't know if devotional is the right word, but a type of spirituality that would not be really what a monk should be, and then how to express that. It's hard. It's not easy to figure out how to do things today. It's just not at all easy! And my job would be to keep the tradition alive, but these are principles that can be applied to any age, any year, any decade, and my job would be to keep this tradition alive and living. I think the community's job — along with the abbot, working together — is to try to express this tradition in a contemporary way: "How are we going to express our poverty today?" Quite different than how we expressed it fifty years ago, but it's still poverty. So it's not so much becoming liberal and wide open, because as long as you try to be poor, you're not loosing your orientation. You may be somewhat not sure about how to be poor sometimes, or maybe you do hit and miss, or do it the wrong way. So that's kind of a little different focus.

When I became superior I introduced what was called the "principal of subsidiarity," which is now quite common. That is, if something can be handled on a local level, let that person do it and not interfere too much. The problem is really a hard one in terms of losing one's "self," because from one point of view, you seem to be expressing your "self," and from another point of view, you've got a job where you can take initiative — you can assert yourself — you can do it the way you think it should be done. Well, that's not an easy thing. The attitude, I think, is dependent upon such things as first, "Am I really trying to do a good job, or am I just trying to push my 'self'?"

In other words, I might say, "I'm abbot now. I really want to serve the community. How am I gonna make a name for myself?" I could be settin' the tables in the dining room and I could say the same thing: "I really wanna do a nice job. I'm gonna set these tables like no brother ever has before, so the community will realize that finally they got somebody who knows what he's doing." It's an attitude.

Another element I think enters in is that we're all in various stages of development — both psychological and spiritual — and before you can give things up, you've got to have something to give. Before you can deny yourself, you gotta have a "self" to deny, which means you've got to do certain things to gain a certain sense of accomplishment.

So I think in the monastery there's a lot of jobs where we do things as *part* of our growth. We *can* assert ourselves, we *can* use initiative, we *can* get a certain sense of pride. And maybe from one point that's not very monastic, but God's grace is a process of growth, and eventually God's grace will come along so that as we get older we are able to give up and say, "Well, I really don't have to do that anymore, so that has been a healthy thing. At the end of the process, I'm still a monk; I'm still happy, I'm still doin' what I think I should be doing," and so then it's all part of a growth.

I think in the past we used to enter the monastery and think, "I have to be obedient, so I won't do anything *unless* I'm told." Well, that's kind of an unhealthy pacifism. In the long run, I think that was destructive. You created attitudes that weren't very good. You see what I'm trying to say there? We all are at some level where we may be all right *here*, but at this *other* level we gotta grow.

Part of the Trappists' way of life is a strong, what they call *cenobitic*, or a strong community influence. Much stronger than a lot of other religious orders 'cause we're cloistered. We're here together all twenty-four hours every day, seven days a week, fifty-two weeks out of the year. And this strong community life does have real *ascesis*, or a strong influence on how we act. We either have to be — I hate to use the word "in step" — but we either have to be working with the community and supporting the community, or we are gonna lead ourselves into a tizzy.

I think many monks get to the point where they realize that possibility of totally becoming just unglued. 'Course, it's probably the *image* we have

Father Thomas says his first Solemn Mass on December 22, 1958.

of ourself coming unglued, you know, we thought, "This is how I want to be and I'm not being that way."

I don't remember the date, but I remember the time of day and the place where I made that choice. I was very keen, and I thought I'm gonna go insane if I stay here, and I thought, "I'll have to go insane." And I really meant it!

I was already a priest, and I felt that I had two options: insanity or sanity. I wasn't too sure which way it was going to go. And I think — I don't know — but I've talked to a number of people and I think frequently they get to that point, the bottom of the barrel. I don't know if everybody gets there or not, so I'm not making any general statements, but I've talked to other monks who have. And I got to that point. The way I resolved it was I decided that, "Well, I'm gonna do God's will. I believe He called me here. I'm going to have to work out my problems in a monastery. If I go insane I'll just have to go insane." I kind of kicked over to the spiritual dimension. So it was a kind of openness to whatever God wanted.

As painful as it was, I really was stepping out of my situation [at New Clairvaux] and getting a little distance, and that pulled me through. Again, the problems didn't go away the next morning — it took a number of years — but at least at that particular moment I set myself in the right direction; I realized that a change of vocation wasn't going to change *me*. I had to change inside, and this was the result.

It's . . . . [pause]. You don't know *who* you are, and then my point of reference is surrender to God, and God hasn't deceived me, and that's important. Now, I don't know about other people how they solve it, 'cause I think God responds to how we're gonna kick in to do it. But I'm glad I didn't run from it because I think I would have gone wacky!

See, we were talking about the "no self." Now to me, a person who then begins to live the rest of his or her life out of that moment — of putting it in higher hands and really surrendering — I think that person is beginning to operate into the "no self," regardless of what he or she does. You can boss everybody around for the next fifty years, but you gotta be careful you don't do it with maliciousness or purely an ego trip. I think that a person who has really integrated himself has, in a way, moved into that "no-self" dimension.

After a certain maturity we attain an integration; we do experience a kind of freedom. In other words, I don't have to push my life in the same way as I left it in terms of rules and things like that. Now, I can't throw everything overboard — I'm not saying that — but there is a type of freedom there, and I think that a person who has reached this point of feeling *total disintegration,* and then succeeding to survive it, moves into a kind of a freedom that *is* a "no-self," and that's where I use the term "no-self." And he kind of lays things out like this.

Then the highest form of integration is the lover, where you just go out of yourself completely into the beloved, which is, of course, perfect, because if you're so hung up on yourself you can't give yourself totally, whether it's in marriage or to God — or God in marriage — or your life or the community or whatnot. So the "no-self" is not an idea of saying, "I have to be kind of lifeless or totally bla. I can't do anything." It's working so that it's not an egotistic way, but in a selfless way; an altruistic way, so to speak.

I have a very incarnational approach to God, and what I mean by that is the more I experience a certain inner peace and contentment, I take that as a good indication that something's happening in my relationship to

God, that we've got a relationship going together. Now, I believe God is manifested very much through my life using creative participation of God's life. Well, I don't know what Gods' life is like. The only way I can know what God's life is like is what *my* life is like. I may be suffering, I may be having a lot of tension and troubles, I'm not saying that everything is peaceful. I may be in a very difficult situation psychologically and exteriorly, but underneath all of it — or in the midst of all of it — there's something saying to me, "No, this is all right. Be at peace. This is okay. This is part of human life and you're doing a good job."

I don't know how to verbalize that feeling. I just *know* that this is the right thing to be doing, that I'm not victimized by it. To me, that is the beginning of, I would say, a real good relationship between me and God — *my* approach to God.

Today there's so much talk about functional and dysfunctional families and persons. The more I feel myself as a functional person, the more I feel that God and I are united — we're one — and I can be a functional person in very difficult situations. I'm not saying that everything's peaceful in my life. You know, the world can be falling down around me, but there's this inner strength. I don't always feel that functional [laughing], and I try to look at my life — my relationship to God — in terms of being more and more steadily a functional person. You know, there'd be more periods when I'm functional than dysfunctional, if I can use that terminology, and then that's where the challenge comes along: "How I'm gonna live my life." I mean, trying to have honest relationships — as difficult as it may be — and not running from situations. Now you're getting into the application of it. But the experience is one of integration, or almost the exact opposite of this disintegration, of this going insane experience.

In being in the monastery here, I obviously have a very ideal situation from my point of view seeking God. But at the same time, there can pop up in my life all kinds of sexual temptations, all kinds of desires, all kinds of ambitions — all kinds of stuff! Now, I've got all that stuff there. Fortunately, because of the situation I'm in, they don't get out of control. When they do get out of control, it gets terribly confused. I've got to work through all of this to get down to experience of the real "self," and it's almost impossible. *It's almost impossible!* My question is, somewhere in the midst of all this — unless a person is really, really malicious — I think there's an element of good, and I think God cuts through all this stuff and gets to that good. And to me, they go to heaven.

Well, I have my own theory. I've thought of that an awful lot. I've looked at all the people that have lived since the beginning of time. Millions! 'Course, I guess we really never know what's on the other side of death, but my theory — I don't know if it holds water, 'cause I've had very limited experience — is I kind of hook onto the element of good that down at the heart of our life there is a desire for good. I think the person whose life seems to be wasted, if there's that basic desire for good influences, and the formation of conscience and behavior — regardless of how big or small it might be — I think that will carry the day through.

If a person commits suicide, they're so distraught for the most part that they don't know what they're doing. That's not the real "self" working there. Now, I know the question of free will gets involved in that. You know, perhaps they *made* a choice. I don't try to sort it out too much, because I feel most people, that the choices they make may not be as good as they think they're making. Or, what do I want to say? May not be as, well, they *think* they're doing the right thing and they're really not. But the mere fact they think they're doing the right thing shows they're kind of in touch with their good. Now a person who's really malicious, well, that's a different situation. A person going around shooting people maliciously: either he's real crazy, in which case he's not responsible, or there is some responsibility there and he'd better get himself straightened out.

I think at some point, certain people would have to make a kind of choice beyond which maybe there's no point of return. But I would say the actions of a person can somewhat reveal that many times these people that you thought wasted some of their life on, say, drugs, I could still question their point of responsibility. I would have no problem in saying that their basic element of good is still there. We really can't judge, because only God knows that, and to me, I don't want to say it's all right to go out and have sex and drugs. I'm not saying that. I'm saying that their goodness, to me, is still basically there, and that's what's going to be their salvation when they stand before God.

It hasn't been easy, I'll agree, but I don't feel cheated at all in my life. *I don't feel cheated at all!* And I think that had I not . . . . Well, if I had embraced another type of life before I entered the monastery — say that I waited until I was twenty-eight to thirty-five — I feel that maybe I wouldn't have done such a good job as I've done in the monastery. Of course, I kinda knew what I wanted, and I don't feel I have made a mistake. If I had it to do over I'd do the same thing.

✝   ✝   ✝

David Rosenberg

Postulant - Entered March 24, 1991

When I first met David Rosenberg he had been in the monastery only a few weeks. As I watched him in church over the course of a few days, I saw a young man deeply engrossed in what is commonly referred to as the "honeymoon period" of the monastic life; those first few months or even years when the novice experiences a blissful-like relationship with God. Of course, as we have learned, this honeymoon eventually ends where all honeymoons must: the reality of day-to-day life for the long haul.

Through David we get the viewpoint of a man fresh from the world who has entered this other realm so totally foreign to him. Expectations and first impressions of the monastic life are new, offering a spark of passion that each man who ever became a monk once encountered at the beginning of his journey into monasticism.

I come from a wealthy family. We've always had everything we needed. I never had to work, and that made me feel sort of incomplete, like there was something more to it than just that. I did the dating and all the normal stuff except work. My parents would give me what I needed, and I sort of had it made, but I felt I was being deprived of something more meaningful. I didn't feel like I was doing the right thing. It's just that perhaps I had grown tired of having so many things, and I always felt a pull towards something nameless — which I didn't know at that moment.

I was in the Christian Brothers College in the Philippines, taking psychology and business management. I went into college just because it was the thing everyone else was doing — I didn't know what I wanted. I can't really say I left the Church, but I stopped during my teenage years basically because of the way they put Jesus and God into my head. They didn't do it in a very gentle way. It was sort of forced upon me; the all-seeing eye, the judge was always watching and was gonna punish you if you did something bad. Sort of the Santa Claus-type, you know, "You better watch out, you better not pout," and I got fed up with that and had to leave the Church in order to find it again. And when I came back with new ignorance, it just took on a whole new meaning, and I had to give myself completely because I was just flooded with the realization that God made us and we will eventually end in Him.

I used to think of this very abstract, very cosmic image of God, you know, this impersonal mass of heaving light, but I couldn't relate to that. In a way, you have to balance the human God and the all-powerful God, and it just comes together in Jesus. I was searching for something I didn't know, which meant I had to reach out a lot to people; to priests, to teachers. I happened upon some Thomas Merton books in '87, '88: *The Seven Storey Mountain* and also *The Sign of Jonas*. That's how I first encountered the Cistercians. I had applied at Our Lady of the Philippines, which is a monastery in Guimaras Ilo Ilo, in the Philippines, and they wouldn't take me because I was eighteen and they said I was too young.

I went to the Carmelites, and the director told me, "You're searching for a deeper intimacy with God, and why don't you go see the Trappists," which I did. Once I saw their way of life and I experienced it for a few days, I knew that was it! I mean, the Cistercian concept of life for God was so total. The giving was without compromise, no vacillating.

They told me to wait seven years in the Philippines because the age they accept is 25 and above, and I was 18, so right away I lived a monastic style of life at home. I made my parents get rid of the maids, the drivers, and the gardeners. The first two years they didn't take me seriously. They thought I just wanted to get out of school and bum around. But when they saw that I was staying home, doing stuff around the house and going to Mass every day and serving in church, they sort of kept quiet. I knew what I wanted and what I had to do. So for three years I did that, and I guess I was a little impatient.

Those three years at home I was basically by myself and with my family and a few friends who stuck it out with me, who were really true friends and didn't care what changes I was going through or how it affected them, 'cause it did affect them. I could see, in a mixed-up sort of positive way, they *did* think a lot more about their faith and their relationship with God.

I didn't feel I had to justify my vocation. These friends I'd go out with on Saturday nights and drive around with, they just thought it was some spiritual phase I was going through. They said, "Oh, you'll be back. You'll see." And it's a sad thing, too, 'cause these are people you love and you see them in that little island which is the world, which they enjoy so much and which I enjoy so much. It's like they don't want to break out, and you ask yourself why.

I caused a lot of unease. It's like Christ who said, "I didn't come here to make everything okay; I came here to create division." It got to the point for awhile as to "what words to use in my presence." It got to be too much. They thought I was this sort of saint, and they were not being themselves. It's the way they see a monk; they think he's a guy who walks on his knees and has his hood on all the time and is doing prostrations, and it's not like that.

So I wrote Our Lady of Joy, which is the monastery in Lantao, Hong Kong, which I've been to quite a few times during our vacations in the Philippines, and I applied. They said they were willing to take me, but they couldn't give me formation because they're quite an old community and they don't speak English very much, they speak Mandarin. So it was their suggestion for me to check out Our Lady of New Clairvaux, and when I heard it was in California I said, "I don't want to go [laughing] to California," because I had this preconception that California was a wild place, like L.A. or something like that. My family moved here last year, and I found out if we're here in California I might as well check it out — have a retreat — and when I came here I found myself knocking at the door and asking to stay. Father Paul Mark thought I was serious enough.

I'm a postulant, and I'll be a postulant for a year before becoming a novice for two years. I do whatever they tell me to do [laughing]. It's that simple. It's fun — fun is a very good word. I think people have this idea that it's a very solemn, very serious and dull place but it's the total opposite. It's exciting, it's happy, and there's just so much freedom, you know, they take care of you. And through obedience, you're free from yourself. That's the way I see it, anyway. I'm not chained to things I want to do or I'd like to do; I just do what comes to me today, and once it's done, it's done.

Before coming here I thought we'd be very silent and very impersonal. I was prepared for that because all of the books I had read were from the fifties and forties, and I wasn't very prepared to witness the changes that have happened in the sixties and seventies. I was pleasantly surprised when I got here and I found that the monks were able to communicate a little more, which gives it a more human aspect to life. It doesn't mean that they can talk all the time, but they can share whatever they're feeling. Another thing I became aware of when I got here was that the life is very balanced, not only between the people but between

No more home cooked meals and fast food! David grabs a glass of milk prior to entering the refectory for a communal meal.

the monks and the environment. We feed on the land. It feeds us and we take care of it, so the oneness is not only between persons but between the environment, too. And in a strange way, I feel I can see the world in a clearer way, and I can even love it when I'm in this frame of mind. It's very open-minded.

The monks made me feel very much like a member of the community. They wouldn't stand back and stare. They were very warm, open, and they liked to show me around, but no one tried to preach or give their own version of the life. They respect the formation of the beginners. And later on, when I have more stability, then they'll be able to share more with me. There's a rule, you know, I'm not supposed to be in contact or to be speaking with the professed unless it's a work-related conversation. We have separate washrooms. We don't usually communicate with them for three years. It doesn't mean we're totally silent; we do bump into each other and say, "Hey, how you doing?" and that's about it. There *are* exceptions, 'cause we have these picnics three times a year. You can walk and talk.

I've been here over a month, and I feel I just got here three days ago. I wear a watch, but I rarely look at it. We're led by the bells. When the bell rings, it either means work is ended or we're being called to church for the Divine Office, and even the bells take on a whole new meaning. When the bell rings you drop everything you're doing — whether it's work or you're writing home, or writing in a diary or even praying — you just drop it and rush to church to meet God. So every time we go to the Divine Office, it's a reaffirmation of the totality of love we have for God.

It's not like coming into an enclosure. Once you go in, everything opens up, and at this moment in time I cannot picture or visualize myself going back into that monastery out there [in society] which is *really* an enclosure. I mean, that's what the world is, and you have to have very strong faith and a very strong vocation and a great love for God if you're called to live and love in the world. Many people think you gotta be a spiritual acrobat to be a monk, and I think it's the opposite. It's much harder out there [in the world]. It's harder to be a parent. I know, because I see how much my parents struggled to bring up the kids and the vocation of husband and wife. Boy, that's hard, and here I am feeling very free, very happy and I just can't believe it!

One thing I *can* say is that it's been easy to let go of the physical stuff: the food, the clothes I like, records and the books. What's hard to let go of is the idealism — the internal habits, ways of thinking — things like that. There *is* a struggle, but when you know who you're doing it for and where you're going and where you're at, it isn't too hard. I mean, things go wrong but that's part of it. It's a whole concept of integration. You don't *try*, because the moment you *try* to do something it gets personal, you see, you start to do something individual. So you just let go — that's the best way I can put it — and be moved by what the community wants, what the director wants.

There's always something that has to be done — whether they verbalized it or not — there's always some charitable thing to do. And sometimes, when there's nothing to do, that's what you *have to* do; you have to do *nothing*. I think a lot is learned more on a wordless level in the presence of the community together at prayer, and just doing things in silence working together. Father Paul Mark is our spiritual director and he's our novice master. He literally has our souls in his hands.

Community is a very strong factor which brought me here, you know.

David tugs at one of the monastery time keepers.

We're in love with God together and it's easier that way. I don't think I could really survive outside by myself, no matter how devoted I was, because you're in the midst of distractions, the rush of people and jobs. I'm not saying everyone has to rush to the monastery to know God. It's just that some people feel a need for recollection and getting away from things in order to find Him, while others are called to work in the city and bring up families. That's a vocation, too.

Out there [in society] — and I hate saying "out there," but for the sake of conversation — it's like we want to have a reality, so we have fashion and we have movies and we have things that are tangible that we can touch and feel and give us security. And when we come here it's like we're going into the unknown, and we're leaving everything we knew, which is

A never-ending supply of monastic leaves.

not easy 'cause when you leave everything, what do you have? We don't know, but I guess we go on a sort of gut instinct, which I like to think is love. And you know, it's a leap of faith. I think that's the difference.

The "world" is a concept; it's a state of being. You can come here [the monastery] and still have the world. Actually, some people bring in the world to the monastery, but to be part of the world is like taking a stance and saying, "I'm self-sufficient: I have my pleasures, my job, my schedule," and they don't see they're being ruled by them. I mean, they *have* to go here, they *have* to go there, they *have* to have their money on the 15th, and they *think* they're doing stuff. The way I see it, it's like they're doing stuff for the money.

People there [in society] are afraid. They're afraid of death, afraid of what's after this temporary scenery so they build monuments, make paintings, and consumerism is such a big thing. It's like they want you to have landmarks and posters — constant reminders of where they are and why they're there. In here, we get rid of all that 'cause we don't want to be anchored, and we don't know where we're going but we just plunge in. It's the life of faith.

In a way I don't feel right now the need to be too aware of world events, though I think it's a good thing the brothers do that because we didn't come here to forget what goes on. That's quite unreal, I think, to ignore what's happening in reality at the moment. So once in awhile I check out the headlines, but I still don't feel a need to get consciously involved. I concentrate more on what I have to learn right now from the books they give me and all of that.

God overwhelms me very much, but no anxiety. If I feel lonely sometimes, I'll feel lonely and that's it. Whatever He brings upon me, I take because it comes from Him, and so in a way it's a constant happiness because you're doing what He wants. When you feel bored, you just offer Him your boredom and say, "God, I'm bored, praise be to you [laughing]." And everything, see, the *totality* is not only the work and the prayer that we give Him, it's every little moment of life; every breath. The *totality* is what I find so attractive in the Cistercian way of life.

It's very intimate to actually *live* a real relationship with God. He's become very tangible, very real, especially in the persons of my brothers. You feel God's love in the most ordinary things. You feel it in creation around you, in your emotions, especially in the circumstances that happen every day: you do something nice for a brother or a brother does something nice for you. It sort of speaks to you of what's going on behind the scenes, how God's moving stuff.

It would be very easy to hide behind an attitude of sanctity and penance. This could be a refuge of sorts, but you'd be fooling yourself, and a lot of people come here, I think, to be safe. It's the total opposite; we come here to be exposed, to face the ugliness and the beauty of who we are together and as individuals. The beautiful and the ugly side, which again makes a *totality*.

Many people leave. I don't know if I will. I mean, I've seen a lot of negative traits in my own personal life, but you have them when you're here and you have them there [out in the world]. The difference is when you come here you see them all the time, it's like they're magnified — you're forced to face yourself. When you're in community, a lot of imperfections are revealed in yourself and in your brothers. I know I have my own little quirks.

I wouldn't know what life would be if I wasn't in love with God. I know the thirst will never be quenched, I've accepted that. I didn't come here to be fulfilled. This is a *means* to an end. I didn't come here *as* an end.

After spending some twenty months at Our Lady of New Clairvaux, David Rosenberg decided to leave the monastery in 1992. The second part of this interview was conducted in October of 1998, six years after his departure from the monastic life. David reflects on his monastic experience and how it has affected his reentry into society to this very day.

I stayed about a year and eight months, almost two years, and then I decided to leave. It's a very intense life. It might seem very slow, very passive from the outside, but they live a much more intense and deeper life than — at least *I* think — we do on the outside. We move amidst a lot of distractions. We have a lot of entertainment; a lot of comfort. We don't have to think much or feel much about what goes on at the soul level. While here in the monastery — and I remember this very clearly — you meet yourself every minute, every instant during the day. The moment you're, let's say, pruning one of these trees and the bell rings because you have to go to church, and you tell yourself, "Oh God, I'm almost done with this tree. Why can't I just finish up here?" And you feel *your* will, you know, *your* selfishness just wanting to unleash itself. But no, you have to put the machine down and you have to say, "Whatever *You* want, Lord," and then run all the way to church.

When you're in the world you don't have that. You want an iced tea, you go have an iced tea [laughing]. Anything! That's why we're kind of like walking in the air out there in the world, missing out on the deeper aspect of life. In the monastery, it's like living under a magnifying glass; everything seems much more intense.

Before I came to New Clairvaux I had read a lot of Thomas Merton books, and I came here with very big illusions: total silence, penitence and all this. When it didn't turn out that way I was quite glad that I stayed because I didn't come here for the *image* of the monastic life. I really wanted to try it out and to see if I was capable of doing it, and in the process I discovered *who* I was.

Not too much has changed from the David Rosenberg back then and the one that's here now. One thing that has changed is that I came here looking for answers — I felt kind of lost — I thought that the answer was monasticism; solitude, the communal life and all this. For some reason I just wanted to be told what I had to do, I wanted to have my normal schedule and get up at a certain hour. It's like there would be no surprises in that kind of life, and that's what I was running away from, the unexpectedness of my life. Life always throws something your way, or God throws something your way to test you or to see how you will react. I thought that by entering a monastery and living this life with your schedule all planned out, I would diminish the number of surprises life would throw my way.

I guess I got my answer, and the answer is that there are no definite answers in life. This is it! *This* is the answer: live *this* way! And I realized after my year and eight months here that I was actually looking for answers, because I felt very insecure about myself, my past, and I realized that I was running away, and I didn't want to become *that* kind of monk; a monk who was running away from the world in order to establish himself in a secure lifestyle in the daily routine. The moment I saw that, I said that I had to change, and it's unavoidable. The moment you realize something, you're already acting. The moment I saw that I was a person who was running away, I changed, and I said, "I have to go back. I can't hide away from it here."

And that's not to say that the other monks are doing that. The other monks are living beautiful lives here. They decided to move forward and discover life inside this place. I just thought about going back to the place where I had escaped from and facing whatever I had to face there. So I spoke to Father Paul Mark. I told him what I felt, I told him that if I was going to become a monk I wanted to become a real monk, not a person who took this option because it seemed the safest.

It was very sad for me because on the selfish level I thought I could make it. On the other hand, I felt that I became a failure to Father Paul Mark and to Father Thomas, who were the two authority figures for me; people I really, really looked up to, and I felt that I had disappointed them. I just felt lousy for about three months just thinking about, "Aw, God! Father Thomas — what must he be thinking about me now? And Father Paul Mark, after all the spiritual guidance he gave me, how could I have betrayed him this way?" And then little by little it just dissipated and I went on with my life.

It was a shock to go back to the world [laughing]. It was strange. What amazed me the most was the speed of things: everybody walked faster, spoke faster, people drove faster. In fact, now that I'm here on retreat, when I speak to Father Paul Mark or Abbot Thomas, it seems to me like they're speaking really slow, and I guess I haven't realized yet that I'm the one who's going too fast, and it's part of the lifestyle outside. You know, you have to make decisions very quickly on the spur of the moment: "I've gotta pay my rent so I've gotta work this much this month," etc.

Getting a job in which there would be a lot of contact with people at all levels is another surprise. Just being in the world is a surprise to me;

being in a traffic jam, being in the office till eight at night, getting home at nine, having dinner really late at night, paying bills and all this — it's not what I like to do for the rest of my life, but it's what I'm doing now.

What surprised me the most was *myself*, and how I wanted desperately to make other people see and feel what I had discovered here. And of course that was wrong, and it was a big lesson in humility to walk around in the midst of speeding people — successful people, people stepping on each other's heads just to get on top — and carry this tiny silence, this tiny bit of monastery inside and not be able to tell anyone about it — not even your closest beings. It's a very humbling experience when you're allowed to be in the presence of God. It kind of goes with it that you cannot share it, and you can't.

I left the monastery in 1992, and I met my wife in February of 1994, and between the day I left and the day I met her, I never went out with anyone else. In fact, I was not interested. I basically had my life planned out. I said, "I'm going to get myself a job, perhaps write poetry or go into language instruction, and I'll just live in solitude." But lo and behold, it's not what one wants but what God wants. And again, it was another lesson in humility: "David, it's not what *you* want. It's whatever will come your way. *His* Will be done."

We fell in love in like one minute! It was at the house of my parents. It turns out that they were friends of my family, and they came over for dinner. It was very romantic; we had the fireplace going. We just looked at each other and it was amazing. I mean, everything I had planned out just vanished right there. Right then and there I said, "Here's my life partner," and she felt the same way, 'cause we told each other this a couple of days later.

She had never met a monk. She thought it was strange at first; she thought I was very passive, that I was too patient. I would sometimes stare into space or look at a tree for half an hour, and she would wonder, "Why is he looking at that tree [laughing]?" I would always tell her, "Well, that's just monastery stuff." I would never really go into it, but I made it a point that after marrying Sandra I would bring her here to have her meet the monks and see where I lived. And we did that. On our honeymoon, we spent one night here, and she fell in love with the place and with Father Paul Mark and Brother Francis and Father Thomas.

I miss some of what I lived here, of what I learned here. I think I'm a more open-minded person because of Our Lady of New Clairvaux. I mean, things can go wrong and I'll take it placidly. And although I have part of it in me at work — I work at this language instruction company and have about fifteen teachers working under me — the pace kills you. You have to be on top of the payroll and billing and driving to work and back home; there's just a thousand things going on in your mind as compared to living here, where the one thing on your mind is — well, at least in *my* mind when I was here — was "How do I reach God? What can I do today to get closer to God?" And that's what I miss. I feel like I'm living a life now that's full of distractions — these different pressures from all sides — and I actually needed to come here for this retreat. I kind of like to reenergize my batteries because I was very tired.

Something very beautiful that I learned here was that communion with the Trinity does not necessarily mean forgetting yourself in bliss or it's not a completely mystical moment. You can be, as Father Timothy says, planting tomatoes and then feeling the sweat drip down the nape of your neck — feeling very hot and uncomfortable — and yet be in prayer or in the presence of the Trinity. That's something I learned here; you should not have any preconceptions about what union or communion means, because the moment you say "It's gotta be this way," then you've lost it. And if you think you *have* it, you lose it, too! It's kind of Zen-like, where the moment is what counts.

Basically what I do now is I leave aside a certain part of each day to meditate or enter into silent prayer, and not necessarily at Sunday mass because the parish life, I would say, completely misses out on this; the mystical aspect of the relationship with God in Christ. And so I carry that little piece of the mystical life — especially as lived here in the monastery — with me, and I cannot share it with anybody at all: *not one person outside of here!* As much as I'd like to, it just makes people look at me in a very confused way, like, "What are you talking about, David?"

When I tell someone that I learned at the monastery to pray without words — it's not a prayer of petition or thanksgiving, it's just to be present in this huge, deep silence that is God — they don't get it, and the more I try to explain it to them or share it with them, it just doesn't work out. So I basically feel that — at least in terms of prayer and relationship with Christ or God — that I'm alone out there. And now being here I feel like I'm in my element again.

It's very difficult for me to go to a normal parish and partake in a regular Mass. It's got to have this deeper meaning; this deeper side to it, and it doesn't. I know that I should be able to adapt to a Mass outside of the monastery, but it's very difficult because you're surrounded by people who feel they *have to* go to Mass on Sunday, they have to kneel at a certain time, and I guess that's one of the marks that the monastery left on me.

I think most people might feel — maybe it's too strong a word — but they might feel afraid to get into this deeper aspect of their religion; the religion they grew up with which is Catholicism, and perhaps it's because they feel safe the way they are right now. You know: "I go to mass on Sunday morning with my wife and kids, and then we go and have breakfast" — whatever. It doesn't go deeper than that. Maybe they feel safe that way, but in real prayer — at least genuine union with God — you realize that you're nobody, you are nothing. He's everything and you are nothing, and I think many people are afraid of that experience to feel that their name, their credit card number, phone number, all their achievements, their position at work — everything — is meaningless in the face of God. And in real prayer you're naked before Him. He doesn't look at your name or your number, it's just you before Him. I don't know if many people would like to feel that way. It's not very comforting, but they cannot be pushed into it. I think the best that we can do is offer people a glimpse, and then it's up to them whether to deepen that glimpse into a longer look or an observation. A few of those might actually want to try it out and get into it. But again, it's not what *we* want; it's whatever God wants. Many are called!

I feel that it's very necessary for me to touch base here all the time. I've gotta come back here. I told my sister, "Whenever I come to California I'll visit my two families: I'll visit you in L.A. and I'll visit my brothers at Vina, because this is very important for me."

✝   ✝   ✝

Epilogue

In reading the lives of these Trappist monks, it becomes evident that certain threads run common throughout each off them. The monks who persevere in the life and remain in the monastery definitely have a special calling from God. It's interesting the manner by which each man was called to the religious life, and even more fascinating the strange detours that some took in arriving at the monastery. The writings of Thomas Merton had an amazing influence in introducing these men to the Trappist lifestyle, and one wonders precisely how many vocations he sparked!

Another predominant element is a period of self-analysis — in some cases psychological disintegration — where the novice or professed monk attempts to discern who he really is. As we've seen, it affects some individuals more than others, but each of them in their own time experiences the pain of piercing through the illusion of the world, and then finding nothing concrete to hold onto except God. This often leads to a crisis of faith, which can rear its head any time within each man's vocation and has a lot to do with whether or not he remains a monk or leaves with a heavy heart.

Perhaps most obvious in these interviews is the absence of bliss or extended periods of actual conscious contact with God. For those who are fortunate enough to experience it, there *are* moments of intense awareness, but a simple day-to-day routine of faith is more typical. The spiritual life, however, is never entered through a casual door. The gate is narrow and intense, and God oftentimes grants the postulant, as Father Timothy said, "a little extra," to get him through those early days. And whether this is a blissful, honeymoon period as some experience, or more of a passion to persevere, eventually this special grace recedes, leaving the monk looking at the long haul with little change of scenery.

I found the Cistercian philosophy on the goodness of mankind to be one of the most attractive traits of the Trappist life. In every case, none of the monks dared to judge any other human being — even Hitler, who probably stands as the epitome of Satan personified. This faith in humanity's basically good nature provides us with a renewed hope for our own salvation by concentrating on the love, mercy, and forgiveness of God, rather than acting as an authoritative judge. The monks don't dismiss the existence of sin or try to rationalize human behavior, but they do possess a more realistic theology with regard to our frailties.

Many readers may wonder if there is more to their community life than what these men have expressed. There always seems to be a truth beyond what is revealed, and when we take a glimpse into the life of any human being, how do we know if we are getting the real truth?

One night shortly before this book was finished, over a couple of beers in the monastery guest house late one afternoon, two monks along with Joe and I talked very openly about truth and the monastic life. Both of these monks have been close friends of ours for over thirty years, and we have seen each other grow in so many stages of personal and spiritual development. And so it was with no undue amount of surprise and disappointment that one of these men, whom I'd originally interviewed in '91, wished to be left out of this book, and wasn't interested in being interviewed again to update his philosophy on the monastic life. His reluctance centered on what he perceived to be the truth, and his feeling hypocritical for talking about spirituality on one level, and not revealing the entire truth about his life at the same time. He feared this imbalance would perpetuate the myth of the holy monk on a spiritual pedestal.

His viewpoint greatly concerned me, and during that visit to the monastery, Joe and I discussed, "What exactly is truth?" Obviously, this monk was experiencing a different take on the life than the others who freely consented to having their interviews published. It led me to another question: "What truth am I presenting about these men, and is it the real truth?"

Joe observed that in society, it seems as though everybody acts as a spin doctor, putting their unique angle on the truth to suit their specific purpose. Whether it be on television or in a court of law, the truth seems to be obscured amidst the confusion caused by those who distort it for one purpose or another. Because God is the *Absolute Truth*, what we humans have devised as truth can be anything, from the *Absolute Truth* to a highly diluted imitation. So Joe and I came to the conclusion that the truth in any given situation probably lies somewhere inbetween the extremes.

I believe what my monk friend was referring to when he questioned the truth was, "What type of spin would this book have? From what angle would I portray the monastic life at New Clairvaux?" This caused me to look at these interviews in a more critical light.

It's a given that we are all sinners, and to one degree or another, hypocrites as well. None of us will ever really know another person, whether you're talking about friends or lovers or monks. There is always going to be a part of the human psyche that we hide from others, and within that abyss lies the root of our personal sinfulness and shame; skeletons that we'd prefer to keep locked within the closet. These ghosts represent the times we have fallen as human beings. That being the case, we shouldn't be looking for a person's dirty laundry because we all could use a trip to the laundromat. What we *should* be focusing on are those facets of a person's personality that they're struggling to keep clean.

You take thirty-five guys with thirty-five different personalities, put them in a community together, add the dimensions of self-analysis and celibacy — which in themselves impart their own inner tensions — and then expect them to pray, work, eat and otherwise live harmoniously in each other's company twenty-four hours a day: *that* is the illusion of monastic life, and that is *not* the truth!

"Truth," notes Father Paul Mark,

> *cannot be simply reduced or equated with all the sordid details of a person's life. But rather, truth cuts through falsehood; all those illusions about life that prevent any human being from developing into what God wants each one to become. Our monastic life is designed to lead us into the Truth — ultimately Jesus Christ — so that our likeness in and to God is restored by grace, which is what redemption is all about. And that truth does set anyone free who is willing to respond to such powerful grace. The stories you have from us are genuine accounts of the search for truth — its cost, its pain. There is nothing false or misleading about them.*

We've learned that one of the goals in the monastic life is to strip away the "self," and turn your will over to God. Each monk at New Clairvaux retains his own personality, that's for sure, and as in any other family, egos can seek their own way and be easily bruised, tempers flare at times when issues become divided, and the unavoidable task of being human gets in the way of achieving spiritual perfection. Yet, we all struggle with this same humanness. It's unrealistic to assume that a man who becomes a monk is immune from all of the pettiness that is inherent in our nature.

Intermingled amidst all of these tensions, the pull from the world to leave the monastery can chase a monk for many years into his monastic life. I've heard of monks who have been tempted to leave the Order in their eighties! Some cross over the hump at a certain stage and become quite acclimated to the life. Others, because of their personalities, may struggle until the day they die, but even if a monk questions the existence of God a million times in his life — and is tempted to leave a million more — the ultimate criteria, in my opinion, is did they persevere, and did they stay? God is going to look at that perseverance and the positive qualities of these men, and judge them within those parameters. The same is true of any of us. All the rest is merely dirty laundry!

I've also observed over the course of time that monks tend to typecast each other, much like an actor who is so identified with one particular role that nobody believes him as another character. Whether this comes from knowing each other too well or not well enough, I can't say for sure, but I do know of one monk in particular who left New Clairvaux after thirty-one years to temporarily help at a monastery overseas. It wasn't until he'd left and lived in a new community as an unknown personality, that he was able to break free of New Clairvaux's perception of him. In his new environment, he could express himself freely without the preconceived notions imposed upon him by his previous community. As a result, he not only grew in the process, but was given a beautiful gift from God of once again being able to see life from the perspective of a child, with all its wonderment at viewing a butterfly or a sunset. It's doubtful this would have happened if he'd never left New Clairvaux, and although he's since returned, there are new facets of his personality that his fellow monks probably will never know.

So with respect to these interviews, they contain the very same honesty and truth by which any one of us would describe our personal lives to a close friend, omitting some of the everyday baggage that we all carry around. And the truth is, that far from being a group of individuals who sit with their legs crossed in prayer all day, these men are merely human beings who are struggling to persevere in their spiritual life the best they can. Their one constant truth is God, and *that* is where they meet in agreement on common ground. Amen.

References

Cistercian History

1. The two main sources of historical facts used for this chapter are the following:

    Thomas Merton, *The Waters of Siloe* (New York: Harcourt, Brace and Company, 1949);

    André Louf, *The Cistercian Way* (Kalamazoo, MI: Cistercian Publications, 1989).

    Quotations taken from each source are noted.

2. Merton, *Siloe*, 5.

3. André Louf, *The Cistercian Way* (Kalamazoo, MI: Cistercian Publications, 1989), 30.

4. Ibid., 32.

5. Ibid., 34.

6. Merton, *Siloe*, 43.

7. Ibid., 54.

Our Daily Bread

1. Thomas X. Davis, *Cistercian Communio* (Vina: Cistercian Studies Quarterly, 1994), Vol. 29.3, 293.

2. Merton, *Thomas Merton On St. Bernard* (Kalamazoo, MI: 1980), 119-120.

3. Louf, *Cistercian Way*, 64, 65, 67.

4. *Constitutions and Statutes* (The Order of The Cistercians of The Strict Observance, 1997), 5.

5. Adam of Perseigne, *The Letters of Adam of Perseigne*, tr. Grace Perigo, intro by Thomas Merton, Cistercian Father Series 21 (Kalamazoo, MI: Cistercian Publications 1976), 39.

6. (Quotation of St. Bernard), Merton, *Thomas Merton On St. Bernard*, 86.

7. Louf, *Cistercian Way*, 76.

8. *Constitutions and Statutes*, 20.

Union With God

1. Bernard of Clairvaux, *On Grace and Free Choice*, tr. Daniel O. Donovan, OCSO; in Bernard of Clairvaux: Treatises III, intro by Bernard McGinn, Cisterican Father Series 19 (Kalamazoo, MI: Cistercian Publications 1977)

2. Bernard of Clairvaux, *On The Song of Songs IV*, tr. Irene Edmonds, Cistercian Father Series 40 (Kalamazoo, MI: Cistercian Publications 1980)

3. Merton, *Thomas Merton On St. Bernard*, 142,143.

4. Ibid., 183.

5. Ibid., 187.

Bibliography & Suggested Reading

André Louf, *The Cistercian Way* (Kalamazoo, MI: Cistercian Publications, 1989)

Thomas Merton, *Thomas Merton On St. Bernard* (Kalamazoo, MI: Cistercian Publications, 1980)

James Finley, *Merton's Palace of Nowhere: A Search for God Through Awareness of the True Self* (Notre Dame, Indiana: Ave Maria Press, 1992)

Thomas Merton, *The Waters of Siloe* (New York: Harcourt, Brace & Company, 1949)

Thomas Merton, *The Seven Storey Mountain* (New York: Harcourt Brace, 1978)

Thomas Merton, *Sign of Jonas* (New York: Harvest/HBI, 1979)

St. Bernard, trans. Paul Diemer, *Love Without Measure* (Kalamazoo, MI: Cistercian Publications, 1990)

M. Basil Pennington, OCSO, *St Bernard of Clairvaux* (Kalamazoo, MI: Cistercian Publications, 1977)

St. Bernard of Clairvaux (1090 - 1153), *Word and Spirit*, a monastic review 12 (Petersham, MA: St. Bedes Publications, 1990)

Etienne Gilson, trans. A.H.C. Downes, *The Mystical Theology of St. Bernard* (Kalamazoo, MI: Cistercian Publications, 1990)

David N. Bell, *The Image and Likeness: The Augustinian Spirituality of William of St. Thierry* (Kalamazoo, MI: Cistercian Publications, 1984)

Amedee Hallier, trans. Columban Heaney, OCSO, *The Monastic Theology of Aelred of Rievaulx* (Kalamazoo, MI: Cistercian Publications, 1969)

John J. Higgins, *Merton's Theology of Prayer* (Spencer, MA: Cistercian Publications, 1971)

Thomas Merton, *The Climate of Monastic Prayer* (Spencer, MA: Cistercian Publications, 1969)

Trans. Benedicta Ward, SLG, *The Sayings of the Desert Fathers* (Kalamazoo, MI: Cistercian Publications, 1975)

Terrence Kardong, *The Benedictines* (Wilmington, DE: Michael Glazier, 1988)

Jean Leclercq, OSB, *The Love of Learning and the Desire for God* (New York: Fordham University Press, 1961)

Louis J. Lekai, *The Cistercians: Ideals and Reality* (Ohio: Kent State University Press, 1977)

Michael Casey, *Sacred Reading: The Ancient Art of Lectio Divina* (Liguori, MO: Triumph Books, 1996)

Kathleen Norris, *The Cloister Walk* (New York: Riverhead Books, 1996)

John Paul II, *Sources of Renewal*, Libreria Editrice Vaticana (New York: Harper & Row, 1979)

Michael Novak, *Confession of a Catholic* (San Francisco: Harper & Row, 1983)

Frans Jozef van Beeck, S.J., *Catholic Identity After Vatican II* (Chicago: Loyola University Press)

Thomas M. Gannon, S.J., editor, *World Catholicism in Transition* (New York: Macmillan Publishing, 1988)

Avery Dulles, S.J., *The Reshaping of Catholicism* (San Francisco: Harper & Row, 1988)

On-Line

For additional books by Thomas Merton and other Cistercian titles, contact *Cistercian Publications* at: http://www.spencerabbey.org/cistpub/

To learn more about the Cistercian life and Trappist monasteries, contact *Cistercian Order in the USA* at: http://www.cistercian-usa.org/usdev.htm

Index

Index

Index

Rosenberg, David, postulant
(New Clairvaux), 31, 43
interview, 176-189

Sacramento, California
arrival of monks from
Gethsemani, 9, 38, 150

San Francisco, California
103-104, 151, 155, 158

Seattle, Washington, 114

Sext, 19, 24

Sheen, Fulton, 54

Sign language, monastic, 153

Southern Pacific Railroad, XVII, 9

Stanford, Leland, XIV, XV, 9

St. Aelred, 76

St. Albert's College, Oakland, CA
105, 109-111, 115
(See also *Dominicans; Father
Anthony.*)

St. Athanasius,
The Life of St. Anthony, 1

St. Augustine, 76

St. Augustine High School,
San Diego
Brother Francis, 85

St. Basil, 76

St. Benedict
Rule of St. Benedict, XVIII, 3-5
8, 17, 77, 87, 92,
127, 132, 137
Rule for Monasteries, 2

St. Bernard, 4, 14, 19, 76
Grace and Free Will, 27-28
The Degrees of Truth, 96

St. Berno, 3

St. Dominic's Parish, Benicia, CA
Father Anthony, residency, 112

St. Dominic's Parish,
San Francisco, California
Father Anthony, 103

St. Meinrad's, monastery, Indiana
Thomas X. Davis, 163.

St. Pachomius, 1

St. Paul, 28, 87, 96, 129

St. Peter, 95

St. Therese, *The Story of A Soul*, 87
Brother Francis, 93

Subiaco, 2

Sunsweet, 42

Tabennisi, 1

Terce, 19, 21

Tibetans, 142

Transcontinental Railroad, 9

U of California, Berkeley
Father Anthony, student, 111

Valley Falls, monastery,
Rhode Island, 136

Vatican II, XVII, 60, 86-87, 111,
169

Vespers, 19, 25

Viet Nam, 92, 154

Vigils, 19, 21

Villa Nova Prep School, Ojai, CA
Brother Francis, 84

Vincentian Fathers
St. Louis, Missouri
Brother Paul Bernard, 136

White Monks, 126

World War II, 8

Young Christian Workers
Father Anthony, member, 102-
104

Zen, 142

201

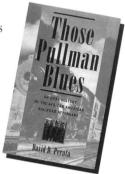
